From Penthouse To Public Housing

Trump, Mamdani, And The Battle Over The American Dream

GEW Social Sciences

Global East-West (London)

Copyright © 2025 by Gew Social Sciences

Prefaced and Edited by Hichem Karoui.

Global East-West (London).

All rights reserved.

No portion of this book may be reproduced in any form without written permission from the publisher or author, except as permitted by copyright law.

Contents

Preface by Hichem Karoui: Zohran Mamdani's Election — 1

1. Origins — 27
2. Defining Success — 43
3. The Housing Crisis — 59
4. Healthcare — 77
5. Immigration Nation — 95
6. Workers and Wealth — 115
7. Climate and Future — 133
8. The Media Wars — 151
9. Winning and Governing — 169
10. America at the Crossroads — 189

Preface by Hichem Karoui: Zohran Mamdani's Election

A Sociological Analysis of the American Dream and Structural Political Realignment

A *masterful analysis of how local politics can challenge national power structures. This book brilliantly captures the tensions between American idealism and structural reality through the lens of one extraordinary election.*

The Mamdani Election as a Sociological Crucible

The election of Zohran Mamdani as New York City's Mayor-Elect in 2025 represents a pivotal moment in the American political sociology landscape. This result goes well beyond mere local change. It serves as a litmus test for two foundational yet often opposing narratives in the Mamdani American mythos. His victory represents a deeply contentious American belief in exceptionalism and upward mobility, otherwise referred to as the American Dream, and the increasing evidence of profound ideological and structural change within the Democratic Party as well as the broad scope of U.S. urban politics.

The Premises Under Examination

This preface ventures forth with the assumption of examining Mamdani's triumph in light of two of the multiple proposals that observers offer. The first is that his rise reaffirms the American core principle of granting access and opportunities to high-purpose endeavours for individuals coming from the most marginalised of backgrounds. The second is that his victory is a glaring indicator of the deeply transformative socio-political state of America, especially concerning the electoral triumph of a self-identified candidate who unapologetically embraced identities and policies considered political 'anathema' in a major U.S. city. The analysis examines and authenticates the facts concerning this rise and dismantles the character and degree of political continuity and systemic rupture that the election represents.

Candidate Profile and Controversial Platform Verification

The sociological analysis deeply relies on constructing the facts regarding Mamdani's identity, platform, and political past. In 2025, Mamdani Zohran is recorded to have taken over for Mayor Eric Adams after winning the general elections for Mayor of New York City. He makes history as the youngest person to be Mayor of New York City, achieving the feat at the age of 34. He's an American citizen, having been naturalised in 2018; he was originally from Kampala, Uganda, to Indian parents. His election as mayor means he is the first Muslim mayor of the city of New York, which is an indicator of increased political representation for people of the city who are Muslims. Before he went on to serve, he was the New York State Assembly member for the 36th district since 2021.

Mamdani holds active membership within the Democratic Party and the Democratic Socialists of America (DSA), describing himself as a democratic socialist. His primary focus on domestic affairs pursued the economics of left-wing populism aimed at tackling deep-seated urban inequality. Aspects of his domestic policy agenda included deep rent control, the provision of certain public services at no charge, such as transit and childcare, and low-income municipal grocery stores. Critically, his platform advocated for aggressively progressive taxation, raising the corporate tax rate and introducing a 2% tax on income over $1 million.

The Stance of Anti-Zionism (The "Anathema")

Mamdani's decisive candidature had an unprecedented approach in all other aspects save one: the stances marked with the most controversy were with regard to foreign policy. On one end of the spectrum, it can be argued that he merely expressed a widely recognised humanitarian principle: "Make no mistake, Israel's military campaign in Gaza is a genocidal war." On the other end, though, there was the unprecedented and potent political campaign one was to expect from a municipal public servant: "I will instruct the New York Police to respect the International Arrest Warrant of Benjamin Netanyahu, issued in November 2024, the moment he steps into New York during my tenure." By extending this argument to the Russian President, Mamdani positioned himself as someone who will defend the logic of international law while also challenging the rationale of American foreign policy that most of the US political class takes for granted and defends so carefully.

This position taken by Mamdani posed a direct challenge to the foreign policy of the United States. People said that he proudly embraced international law, which America routinely overlooked. He became immediately and all too often condemned, with his rivals and some pro-Netanyahu actors even claiming that he was doing the 'most shameful' thing, being a 'Hamas propaganda' apologist, and exhibiting antisemitism by default.

Fact 1: The Complex Reality of the American Dream in the 21st Century

Mamdani finally won, but assessing his win as individual success seems to uphold the story of America being the land where an 'outsider' can attain the apex of civic glory, similarly to Barack Obama before him. However, sociologically, this success story rationalises an extraordinary ideological denial of the foundational capitalist tenets of the American Dream.

Mamdani as the Quintessential 'Outsider' Success Story

Mamdani's life is a true story of an immigrant born in Uganda, a Bowdoin College graduate, a U.S. citizen, and a grassroots activist who, in due course, became the mayor of the largest city in the U.S., and the story is a testament to the enduring relevance of the political dimension of the American Dream. He achieved his goal without "big-money donors or deep political connections." Rather, he relied on extensive grassroots mobilisation to augment his political base. His achievement is clear proof that even in an environment of political polarisation and cynicism, structures that enable social and political ascension are still accessible. He is the city's first Muslim mayor and first holder of African and South Asian heritage. His election underscores the growing political incorporation of people with diverse cultural backgrounds into the American polity.

Whenever the comparison of Mamdani and Barack Obama arises, the achievement of high purpose by a non-traditional candidate comes to mind. However, while this analogy can be advantageous in navigating minority political success, it also highlights a crucial difference in the thought process. Obama's elevation is significant because it stems from a race-driven context and relies on a political tool intentionally designed to Americanise its colour, framework, and fundamental order.

Mamdani's approach is far more distinct than others. His public mandate is anti-capitalist socialism, and he seeks to change the economic structure of the system's hierarchy. If, to some, taxing the rich and advocating for public, collective ownership of core services is an achievement of the American Dream, the analysis indicates that the dream's interpretation has shifted from the standard individualistic, capitalist, economic framework. The positive aspect is that his success validates the American political ideal of accessibility and simultaneously indicates a deep societal disillusionment with the unfettered capitalist economic promise. His achievement confirms the political aspect of the American Dream: access to political power, but with an electoral mandate that seeks and intends to deliver wealth redistribution. The result indicates a transformation of the American, individualistic "dream" to the pursuit of social equity.

Sociological Critique: Class, Inequality, and Identity in the Narrative

The American Dream complex tends to focus more on an individual's effort while ignoring boundaries like socioeconomic, racial, and gender inequality. Mamdani employs sociological imagination with DSA and reframes issues such as the high cost of living as public concerns, which provides a basis for his systemic solutions like universal rent control and free childcare.

His electoral coalition, which received overwhelming support from Black and Hispanic communities, rests on a political calculus that recognises the promise of Americana has been historically conditional. The fight for decades on for racial justice—where communities struggled to attain the status of "first-class citizens" in a marketplace that utilised and rewarded them—demonstrates that political gains for the most afflicted are not the result of singular achievements, but the result of monumental and laborious political attempts to address systemic denial and exclusion. The successful integration of identity politics and class politics has enabled Mamdani to turn his identity as an outsider—a Ugandan, a Muslim, and of Indian descent—into a powerful rhetorical weapon in the fight against the "rich and the powerful" who geopolitically hold the decision-making authority. The complex usage of identity that undergirds left populism adds to the narrative of political mobilisation in the region and provides a compelling counter to the individual merit narrative.

Fact 2: The Normalisation of the Anathema and Evidence of Political Rupture

Mamdani winning the NYC mayoral race despite holding the anti-Zionist position and wearing the Democratic Socialist badge with pride is absolute proof of a rupture within American urban socio-political structures. This result is contrary to most expectations and shows how political taboos are beginning to erode in large metropolitan areas.

The Socialist Mainstream: Ideological Shift in Urban Governance

The appointment of a democratic socialist to the top position in New York City—the premier financial capital of the world—is a profound change in the political culture. The Democratic Socialists of America is a group that, until recently, was considered part of the extreme left wing of the political spectrum. Institutional validation has now established them as the city's centre. Their ideas are now accepted as mainstream. Despite centrists' criticism, their core ideas now hold political viability.

This transformation did not occur due to a change in ideology among the general population. Rather, it results from the successful mobilisation of a dedicated community. Evidence suggests the win was underpinned by a record voter turnout, more than 2 million for the first time since 1969. This extraordinary turnout was a result of strong mobilisation among the progressive and youth voter bases, as noted by the solid support for Mamdani in deep blue districts. This points to what might be described as a turnout-driven "selective enthusiasm" election, not a deep-seated change among the electorate. Still, the outcome of this election indicates a deep political realignment, with the formal DSA endorsement of a self-identified socialist who won a major governing position.

The Post-Gaza Political Reconfiguration and the Shattering of Foreign Policy Taboos

Mamdani's vehement criticism of Israel is the most striking evidence of rupture. The results of the election in NYC show that unequivocal support for Israel, which has long been considered a must-have for serious candidates in American major city politics, especially in New York, is losing its power as a political litmus test. Mamdani's election happened at the same time as other progressive wins, including Ghazala Hashmi's in Virginia, which indicated that public opinion is becoming more important to politicians.

The promise to carry out the ICC warrant against Prime Minister Netanyahu was not just talk; it was a powerful political act of disobedience that showed a commitment to international legal standards over established U.S. foreign policy norms. The media all over the world paid a lot of attention to this point of view, and it sparked a discussion about a possible change in U.S. foreign policy, especially in the Middle East and among progressive movements around the world.

It is striking that, unlike other prominent progressives like Congressman Jamaal Bowman and Congresswoman Cori Bush, whose primary challenges resulted in very visible losses due to AIPAC and other pro-Israel PACs' unprecedented spending in the multi-million dollar range, Mamdani seems to have 'got away' with being anti-Zionist. An in-depth analysis of the causal mechanisms suggests that the 'stunning' capture of the municipal election by Mamdani was a result of central campaign promises addressing the municipal affordability of rent, housing, and childcare. The electorate, especially the working class and youth who were active and energised, put the priority on economic survival. Domestic economic survival was more important to them than the concern of foreign policies. His anti-Zionist position, instead of being perceived as a liability, underwent a transformation and became a positive symbol of opposition to the establishment. This approach is unlike the position of his opponent, former Governor Andrew Cuomo, and the mainstream Democratic Party. These developments resulted in an electoral apparatus in which radical and traditionally 'electoral suicide' foreign policies can be normalised and, in fact, used as a tool to galvanise support, as long as they are strategically placed in the context of a strong, cohesive domestic economic agenda in a densely populated urban area.

The Geographical Limitation of Structural Change

Despite the apparent rupture at the municipal level, the evidence indicates that this structural change remains limited to specific geographical areas. In stark contrast to the obstacles progressives encounter in congressional races, Mamdani has had success. Congressional districts, in stark contrast to the rest of the NYC electorate, are smaller, more frequently ideologically diverse, and far more susceptible to external political spending than the rest of the electorate. For instance, in the primary races to unseat Representative Bowman and Representative Bush, AIPAC's affiliated super PAC funded them with close to $25 million in total.

    The city's context served as a protective layer for local

candidates. For instance, in the NYC mayoral election, which has more than 3.12 million voters, outside groups find it much more difficult to concentrate their efforts and frame a candidate solely as a foreign policy candidate due to the candidate's ability to rally a large grassroots movement of approximately 28 volunteers. A dedicated grassroots base like this makes it easier to rally support. Mamdani's motivated supporters organised the campaign, broadening the support base and diluting single-issue external counter-efforts.

This study indicates that within deep-blue urban confines, the success model of radical platform normalisation is sufficient for ideological preservation and election success, but as of yet, deeply radical transformations remain out of reach for other marginal, geographically diverse congressional districts.

The subsequent table captures and compares the elections, thus demonstrating the impact of priority issues and geography on the success of progressive politics.

Table I: The Contrast in Progressive Electoral Success (AIPAC vs. Affordability)

Candidate	Office	Stance on Israel/Gaza	Outcome	Role of Pro-Israel PAC Spending	Primary Campaign Focus
Zohran Mamdani	NYC Mayor	Anti-Zionist; ICC Pledge to arrest Netanyahu	Won (General)	Minimal/Contained backlash in general election	Affordability, Rent Control, Class Justice
Jamaal Bowman	US House (NY-16)	Criticised Israel post-Oct 7	Lost (Primary)	$20M+ spent by UDP/AIPAC against him	Progressive, Domestic Policy
Cori Bush	US House (MO-01)	Criticised Israel post-Oct 7	Lost (Primary)	$5M+ spent by UDP/AIPAC against her	Progressive, Domestic Policy

The Mechanisms of Change: Coalition, Mobilisation, and Counter-Narrative

Mamdani securing a win couldn't have been considered a coincidence but the result of carefully building a coalition of voters motivated by economic urgency and inspired by a campaign style that was digital and authentic. It showed a changed, sophisticated approach to urban campaigning.

The Demography of Rupture: A Coalition of the Excluded

Mamdani's supporters that enabled him to win were different from the usual establishment Democratic voters in terms of their demographics and their ideology. The youth vote was the most important demographic: young voters aged between 18 and 29 supported him the most with a whopping 78%, making them the strongest base for him compared to any other candidate in this age category. Additionally, the 19% youth voter turnout for this municipal race was an increase in turnout, which confirms the dominance of younger voters in this age group as well as their alignment with progressive and democratic socialist ideals.

Mamdani was able to build a multiracial working class, which enabled him to win by going beyond ethnic and racial boundaries.

His campaign not only witnessed considerable victory margins across several excluded areas but also captured Black majority precincts by 26 percentage points and Hispanic majority precincts by 20 percentage points. This kind of multiracial support is strong and indicates the successful uniting of culturally driven identity politics with class-based economic urgency. That shows the remarkable successes the campaign managed to achieve. It also indicates the remarkable way they supplanted the moderate establishment Democrats and managed to form a solid economic populist union front. The campaign's installation strategies were heavily reliant on energetic and decentralised mobilisation tactics that created an unprecedented volunteer mobilisation of over 100,000 people, along with viral social media engagement with 5.6 million followers on Instagram, TikTok, and other social media platforms to match the unrivalled financial dominance of other candidates, most notably Andrew Cuomo.

The Red-Green Counter Narrative and Ideological Framing

Mamdani's campaign likely planned to utilise the entire social media spectrum to effectively target the younger audience disillusioned with the current political apparatus, thereby avoiding overly complex strategies and instead focussing on tangible plans that address the multifaceted collateral suffering caused by deteriorating social and economic conditions in the city, particularly affecting the working population. This framing of the social and economic situation in the cities and surrounding areas helped mitigate the impact of competing narratives promoted by other candidates and political critics who sought to restrict the campaign's definition to Socialists, Democrats, or extreme foreign policy positions.

Concerning his success, conservative commentators speculated about the victory's meaning by politically branding it the "triumph of a Red-Green'" alliance. This narrative poses the menacing combination of revolutionary Marxism (democratic socialism – 'Red') and Islam (his Muslim identity and pro-Palestinian activism – 'Green'). This narrative is based on historical examples of volatile coalitions that ultimately led to authoritarianism. This criticism attempts to, in particular, diminish the success by equating 'democratic socialism' and 'anti-Zionism' with extremism and theocratic authoritarianism.

Nonetheless, a careful reconsideration of the electoral mandate suggests that this critique from the left, "red-green," viewpoint is a profoundly misplaced characterisation of the electoral process. Mamdani's coalition, it is true, was not purely radical and theocratic but rather was, at its core, economic and pragmatic. Remarkably, Mamdani was able to win more than a third of the city's Jewish vote. Moreover, he also received cross-endorsements from leading liberal Zionists, including the Comptroller Brad Lander and Representative Jerrold Nadler, who, despite differences on the Israel issue, supported his domestic agenda. This is sufficient evidence that the coalition was a class-identity synthesis and was able to achieve a successful bottom-up, cross-aggregated coalition of voters from deeply opposing ideological perspectives on fundamental economic justice. The identity and anti-Zionist components worked strategically to mobilise specific social segments (youth, Muslims, and the progressive left) but did not wholly exclude moderate voters interested in reforms to the city's economic constitution. The framing of the Mamdani coalition by critics, rather bluntly, seems to be an effort to bypass the cross-structural boundaries that underpin Mamdani's achievement as a form of political caution rather than a sincere description of the constituency that secured his election.

Table II: Mamdani's Mandate: Coalition Demographics (2025 NYC Mayoral Election)

Voter Segment	Mamdani Support Rate	Margin of Victory/Data Point	Sociological Significance
Overall Vote Share	50.4%	Highest turnout since 1969 (>2M votes)	Demonstrated the efficacy of grassroots mobilisation over establishment finance in a city-wide race.
Youth Voters (18-29)	78%	Strongest base; 19% youth turnout (major increase)	Confirmation of a definitive generational alignment with DSA/progressive values.
Majority Black Precincts	N/A	Won by 26 percentage points	Successful displacement of moderate establishment Democratic influence among Black voters.
Majority Hispanic Precincts	N/A	Won by 20 percentage points	Successful integration of immigrant and working-class minority groups into the socialist coalition.
Jewish Voters	>33%	Mamdani won over a third of Jewish voters	Evidence that Mamdani's anti-Zionist stance was not a universal litmus test even within the Jewish community.

Institutional Constraints and the Prognosis for Structural Change

Fact 2 analysis - above mentioned- still points to a deep social-political fracture on the ground, which the success of Zohran Mamdani underscores. Simultaneously, the resilience of this change and its complete integration into the framework hinge solely on the ability of U.S. federal and state structures to obstruct or restrain the radical aspects of his agenda.

The Challenge of Governing Radicalism: Local and Financial Constraints

Among many political figures in the world, few are as complex as the one that Mamdani assumes, frequently said to be second only to the president of the United States in political difficulty. The same systemic issues of stagnation, budgetary gaps, and local dominant power systems—in particular, the very real estate and finance blocks—will be barriers to the realisation of the more radical promises of the social system. Even with universal rent control, proponents claim that the system will result in the same housing and capital flight that the city experienced in the 1970s.

In addition, DSA's maximalist position includes prison abolition and the defunding of police as central tenets. The extent to which Mamdani is able to adapt the leftist policing agenda towards the creation of the "Department of Community Safety" will be a defining factor in the sustenance of his political capital. The quicker he attempts to adopt the radical left ideology of his supporters, the more he begins to lose coalition strength. This does not change the fact that the traditional political establishment believes, and will continue to believe, that the rule of socialists is equivalent to chaos.

Intergovernmental Hostility: The Structural Veto

The upper tiers of the state pose the most serious barriers to Mamdani's institutional power, using constitutional and budgetary means to veto and sabotage his plans of action.

The resistance portrayed serves as a protective barrier against radical ideological shifts, which can start at the local level.

During the post-primary elections, the federal sitting president, Donald Trump, called Mamdani the "Communist Candidate" and said that "the city had zero chances of success" and threatened that he would not provide federal money to the city. This threat to cede control of fiscal federalism to the Trump administration represents, in Mamdani's view, a direct and foundational form of violence designed to disrupt and preempt the success of the city, which he aims to lead, in anticipation of the 2026 midterm elections.

Moreover, the federal government carefully designed and planned to neutralise Mamdani's most significant and globally resonant promise. Some members of Congress, such as Senator Rick Scott and Representative Elise Stefanik, swiftly reacted to his promise to apprehend Netanyahu, calling his arrest based on an ICC warrant. This legislative initiative indicates the institutional inflexibility of the federal government to unilateral control over foreign and international policy by the United States, signalling to local decision-makers that they, and the foreign relations in which they are engaged, are subject to the control of the national security agenda.

The limitation of Mamdani's sovereignty is functional: while the electoral system allows a radical candidate to win, the federal system makes sure that almost all of his radical international policy proposals are functionally vetoed or rendered moot. Structural constraints mean that any real, sustainable change Mamdani implements will only pertain to local, domestically manageable policies like state-regulated rent or state-regulated taxation. His term will be the first to exemplify the endurance of federal checks in the U.S. against radical local movements. That the municipal movement is able to provide real economic relief in the face of permissive state and federal obstruction will be the determining factor as to whether the progressive surge translates to a sustained political framework or remains an episodic political surge that has not transformed the status quo.

Conclusion: Mamdani's Legacy in American Political Sociology

Zohran Mamdani's election as Mayor-elect of New York City represents a complex and profoundly enlightening occurrence in American political sociology, integrating two ostensibly contradictory realities.

Synthesis of the Dual Narratives

The evidence presented above illustrates the persistence of the American Dream narrative (Fact 1) in a purely political aspect: the system is open enough for an immigrant, a Muslim, a member of the working class, and an outsider to hold a local chief executive position. Nonetheless, his ideological mandate decisively rejects the core traditional capitalist underpinning of the Dream by advocating for the use of the open system to redistribute economic power and correct inequities through socialist strategies.

More importantly, his election offers a firm confirmation of the existence of a profound, local structural fracture in American urban politics (Fact 2). This fracture is marked by the normalisation of the identity of a democratic socialist and anti-Zionist who, through elaborate grassroots mobilisation and generational activism, has attained hegemonic status. This shift reveals the dynamics of the urban Democratic coalition, where concern for economic justice now serves as an effective shield to protect candidates from foreign policy-based McCarthyite ideological purges.

The prognosis is a hint at the overwhelming difficulty of translating the socio-political rupture illuminated by Mamdani's radical campaign, and the structures they are embedded in, towards deep, enduring institutional transformation.

The prompt opposition from federal and state institutions, especially concerning foreign relations and the possibility of fiscal retaliation, speaks to the readiness of the American constitutional system to contain and restrain the dangerously radical torch of local self-governance. Mamdani's time in office will, therefore, be noted as one of the most important, or rather, a critical experiment: a case study of the ability of a local, bottom-up, class movement to break the systemic, static, and structural dominance of an advanced federal system and transform, in essence, the economic and social life of the world's capital of finance.

Finally, a book that explains why politics feels so different now. The Mamdani story shows us that change is possible, even in the most unlikely places.

Hichem Karoui (8 Nov. 2025)

References For Further Reading

1. Zohran Mamdani's win as New York Mayor shows that America can still be a land of opportunity, accessed November 7, 2025, https://blogs.lse.ac.uk/usappblog/2025/11/05/zohran-mamdanis-win-as-new-york-mayor-shows-that-america-can-still-be-a-land-of-opportunity/
2. How a 'pro-Palestinian' Zohran Mamdani became mayor of 'Jew York', accessed November 7, 2025, https://timesofindia.indiatimes.com/world/us/how-a-propalestinian-zohran-mamdani-became-mayor-of-jewyork/articleshow/125109241.cms
3. Mamdani's New York victory signals shift in US political landscape, accessed November 7, 2025, https://en.yenisafak.com/world/mamdanis-new-york-victory-signals-shift-in-us-landscape-3710281
4. accessed November 7, 2025, https://en.wikipedia.org/wiki/Zohran_Mamdani
5. Live Results: New York City 2025 mayoral election, accessed November 7,

2025, https://www.pbs.org/newshour/politics/live-results-new-york-city-2025-mayoral-election

6. accessed November 7, 2025, https://en.wikipedia.org/wiki/Zohran_Mamdani#:~:text=Zohran%20Kwame%20Mamdani%20(born%20October,elect%20of%20New%20York%20City.

7. Bowdoin Alum Zohran Mamdani '14 Is the Next Mayor of New York City Following Historic Election, accessed November 7, 2025, https://www.bowdoin.edu/news/2025/11/mamdani-nyc-mayor.html

8. Zohran Mamdani wins NYC mayor's race, capping a stunning ascent, accessed November 7, 2025, https://www.opb.org/article/2025/11/04/zohran-mamdani-wins-nyc-mayor-s-race-capping-a-stunning-ascent/

9. Liberal politicians outside US hail Zohran Mamdani victory in New York, accessed November 7, 2025, https://www.theguardian.com/us-news/2025/nov/05/zohran-mamdani-victory-uk-labour-india-israel

10. Zohran K. Mamdani - New York State Assembly, accessed November 7, 2025, https://assembly.state.ny.us/mem/Zohran-K-Mamdani/contact/

11. The Colors of Zohran Mamdani in New York, accessed November 7, 2025, https://grapheine.com/en/magazine/the-colors-of-zohran-mamdani-in-new-york/

12. America is divided into two countries - Trump's pro-billionaires and Mamdani's anti-billionaires, accessed November 7, 2025, https://www.morningstar.com/news/marketwatch/20251106148/america-is-divided-into-two-countries-trumps-pro-billionaires-and-mamdanis-anti-billionaires

13. The Struggle Beyond the Ballot : Understanding Zohran Mamdani's Campaign, accessed November

7, 2025, https://www.cadtm.org/The-Struggle-Beyond-the-Ballot-Understanding-Zohran-Mamdani-s-Campaign

14. NYC mayoral candidate Zohran Mamdani's statement on Oct. 7 attacks deemed "shameful" by Israel - CBS News, accessed November 7, 2025, https://www.cbsnews.com/newyork/news/nyc-mayors-race-zohran-mamdani-october-7-statement-israel/

15. Local Threats, Global Warrants: Mamdani, the ICC, and Constitutional Boundaries, accessed November 7, 2025, https://international-and-comparative-law-review.law.miami.edu/local-threats-global-warrants-mamdani-the-icc-and-constitutional-boundaries/

16. Zohran Mamdani announces all-female transition team as he prepares for New York mayoralty, accessed November 7, 2025, https://www.theguardian.com/us-news/2025/nov/05/zohran-mamdani-transition-team

17. Random Musing: Why Zohran Mamdani will find it hard to be another Barack Obama | World News - The Times of India, accessed November 7, 2025, https://timesofindia.indiatimes.com/world/us/random-musing-why-zohran-mamdani-will-find-it-hard-to-be-another-barack-obama/articleshow/125060895.cms

18. America's Story: An Immigrant Story - Carnegie Corporation of New York, accessed November 7, 2025, https://www.carnegie.org/interactives/immigration-reform/

19. Mamdani win draws celebration on global left, condemnation in Israel, accessed November 7, 2025, https://www.washingtonpost.com/world/2025/11/05/zohran-mamdani-new-york-victory-world-reactions/

20. The Radical DSA and the New York City Mayor's Race - Third Way, accessed November 7, 2025, https://www.thirdway.org/memo/the-radical-dsa

-and-the-new-york-city-mayors-race

21. The American Dream Examined in Literature | Research Starters - EBSCO, accessed November 7, 2025, https://www.ebsco.com/research-starters/literature-and-writing/american-dream-examined-literature

22. The Illusion of the American Dream: How the American Dream Fails to Acknowledge Inequality - Engaged Sociology, accessed November 7, 2025, https://engagedsociology.wordpress.com/2018/04/30/the-illusion-of-the-american-dream-how-the-american-dream-fails-to-acknowledge-inequality/

23. The Surprising Part About Mamdani's Win, accessed November 7, 2025, https://www.city-journal.org/article/zohran-mamdani-black-hispanic-voters

24. Is the American Dream Dead? | UC Davis, accessed November 7, 2025, https://www.ucdavis.edu/magazine/american-dream-dead

25. "The Negro and the American Dream," Excerpt from Address at the Annual Freedom Mass Meeting of the North Carolina State Conference of Branches of the NAACP, accessed November 7, 2025, https://kinginstitute.stanford.edu/king-papers/documents/negro-and-american-dream-excerpt-address-annual-freedom-mass-meeting-north

26. From the Origins to the Present-Day Relationships between the African American Community and the Republican Party - NIH, accessed November 7, 2025, https://pmc.ncbi.nlm.nih.gov/articles/PMC10052273/

27. Black Ethnics: Race, Immigration, and the Pursuit of the American Dream | Oxford Academic, accessed November 7, 2025, https://academic.oup.com/book/7472

28. How Mamdani built an 'unstoppable force'

that won over New York, accessed November 7, 2025, https://www.theguardian.com/us-news/2025/nov/06/zohran-mamdani-campaign-new-york-democrats

29. Behind Mamdani's Revolutionary "Red-Green" Victory Over New York City, accessed November 7, 2025, https://jcpa.org/behind-mamdanis-revolutionary-red-green-victory-over-new-york-city/

30. Democratic Socialists of America - Wikipedia, accessed November 7, 2025, https://en.wikipedia.org/wiki/Democratic_Socialists_of_America

31. Where the vote for Mamdani was strongest in New York City, accessed November 7, 2025, https://www.theguardian.com/us-news/2025/nov/05/mamdani-vote-new-york-city

32. Why Democrats should be wary of over-reading the Zohran Mamdani's New York win, accessed November 7, 2025, https://timesofindia.indiatimes.com/world/us/why-democrats-should-be-wary-of-over-reading-the-zohran-mamdanis-new-york-win/articleshow/125107543.cms

33. Young Voters Power Mamdani Victory, Shape Key 2025 Elections, accessed November 7, 2025, https://circle.tufts.edu/latest-research/young-voters-power-mamdani-victory-shape-key-2025-elections

34. Mamdani Created a Left-Liberal Coalition on Israel/Palestine, accessed November 7, 2025, https://jewishcurrents.org/mamdani-created-a-left-liberal-coalition-on-israel-palestine

35. Mamdani's lesson, accessed November 7, 2025, https://bowdoinorient.com/2025/11/07/mamdanis-lesson/

36. CAIR, CAIR Action Congratulate 38 Muslim Election Winners, Report At Least 76 Muslim Candidates Nationwide,

accessed November 7, 2025, https://www.cair.com/press_releases/cair-cair-action-congratulate-39-muslim-election-winners-report-at-least-77-muslim-candidates-nationwide/

37. Why the progressive 'Squad' is getting smaller after defeats this primary cycle - AP News, accessed November 7, 2025, https://apnews.com/article/squad-aipac-progressives-congress-cori-bush-0de0a96929368db72145b033261415ca

38. Jamaal Bowman's primary defeat leaves progressives angry at role of Aipac - The Guardian, accessed November 7, 2025, https://www.theguardian.com/us-news/article/2024/jun/26/jamaal-bowman-primary-progressives-aipac

39. NYC mayor election 2025: How Mamdani vs. Cuomo's plans for charter schools and Foundation Aid could shape NYC classrooms, accessed November 7, 2025, https://timesofindia.indiatimes.com/education/news/nyc-mayor-election-2025-how-mamdani-vs-cuomos-plans-for-charter-schools-and-foundation-aid-could-shape-nyc-classrooms/articleshow/125099202.cms

40. Democrats sweep key races in 2025 elections in early referendum on Trump, accessed November 7, 2025, https://www.cbsnews.com/live-updates/election-day-2025-voting-results/

41. A Big Win For Now, accessed November 7, 2025, https://www.gmfus.org/news/big-win-now

42. Gotham's Red-Green Takeover: The Mamdani Experiment Begins - Middle East Forum, accessed November 7, 2025, https://www.meforum.org/mef-observer/gothams-red-green-takeover-the-mamdani-experiment-begins

43. Reeher Speaks With AFP, The Guardian, The Hill and Newsweek About Mamdani's Win in NYC, accessed

November 7, 2025, https://www.maxwell.syr.edu/news/article/reeher-speaks-with-afp-the-guardian-the-hill-and-newsweek-about-mamdani-s-win-in-nyc

44. Zohran Mamdani called out Donald Trump's threat to withhold federal funding in New York City- as it happened, accessed November 7, 2025, https://www.theguardian.com/us-news/live/2025/nov/03/us-government-shutdown-donald-trump-latest-politics-news

45. Sen. Rick Scott Introduces Bill to Prevent NYC's Mamdani from Arresting PM Netan, accessed November 7, 2025, https://www.rickscott.senate.gov/2025/10/sen-rick-scott-introduces-bill-to-prevent-nyc-s-mamdani-from-arresting-pm-netanyahu-on-u-s-soil

1
Origins
Contrasting Childhoods and Formative Experiences

The Landscape of Queens: Demographic and Economic Overview

Much like the rest of the world, Queens, the most expansive of New York City's boroughs, contains a unique mosaic of communities and varying levels of economic wealth. These features, along with the economic surges following World War II and subsequent immigration to America, allowed both Donald Trump and Shahidul Alam Mamdani to flourish in New York while still children. In spite of the still rampant inequities and diversity, the obtuse economic shifts Queens was undergoing allowed the children of Mamdani and Trump to develop worldviews of the land and its people greatly different from one another. Moreover, the stark contrasts of neighbourhood compositions in wealth and class allowed these people to develop unnatural views on identity and the privileges the country had to offer. Furthermore, America's immigration phenomena, along with the repeated culture, class, and economic disparities, created a thick molasses that profoundly shaped the worldviews of Mamdani and Trump. These subtleties gave the kids the means to form their own views of the world and America, even in Queens' heavy traffic.

Trump's Upbringing: Affluence and Access in a Thriving Era

Upon Donald's birth, he was welcomed into a well-to-do family and into a thriving America, which indicated that his father's exposure as a successful real estate developer was more than enough to enable Donald to live in Jamaica Estates, a luxurious suburb in Queens. Throughout the 1940s, Queens was considered one of America's most desirable and luxurious suburbs, as well as a beacon of wealth in New York City. Splendid opulent houses, considered the epitome of affluence, embellished the landscape, and thriving stores sat along main thoroughfares. Transport was accessible to the city via the Red Route buses. His journey through Queens was certainly the great American dream, and he had the innate being that suggested that he was born with a silver spoon and destined to be successful in life. This narrative was also endorsed and, in a way, contributed to the idea that the late 1940s up to the mid-1960s to the early 70s was an era. This era is characterised by the period of expansion and affluence achieved due to the incredible economic system that America developed after the Second World War. He also most likely accepted the insatiable appetite that America had for capitalism as something he was born with. This more than likely became a mental frame for him at a young age. Along with the fast-paced changes in the area, capitalism was growing and matched the economy's willingness to nurture optimism in Queens. For such a young age, Donald was conditioned to be an assertive, ambitious individual with strong entrepreneurial instincts. His formative years were embedded in an environment which predominantly fostered this attitude.

He immersed himself in an almost limitless world of possibilities, surrounded by power and influence, from exclusive preparatory schools to high-society engagements. His father's influence and his privileged upbringing had a huge impact. It instilled in him a troubling perspective on the value placed on merit, success, and social class. From the perspective of affluence and opportunity, the years that Trump spent in Queens offer a most instructive context to delineate the genesis of the ethos that would carry him in his pursuits.

Mamdani's Beginnings: Immigrant Roots and Cultural Resilience

Mamdani's youth was nurtured among the rich diversity of immigrants the community was home to, and he settled in Queens. His hard-working and resilient parents had to abandon their homeland to pursue and build a better future and thus educated him on the virtue of cultural grounding and sacrifice. Being submerged in the family's traditional customs and stories, coupled alongside the struggles and navigation of the immigrant population, built in him a strong pedagogical appreciation. Dropping the notions of 'otherness', alongside the warmth of a home filled with traditional dishes and the symphony of the persistent chatter of several tongues, was a space of community, solidarity, and celebration. It was during this enlightenment that a spark of curiosity was ignited in him regarding how people and, for that matter, the entire community, were affected by the distinct absence of social justice. The world supported those seeking social justice, with empathy being the most powerful and essential element present; the central purpose of all his work was to include and empower every individual.

For Mamdani, the mosaic of his community was more than a beautiful sight; it was a lasting homage to the pioneers of imaginative thinking beyond the confines of their birthplace. The harrowing sagas and successes of his immigrant neighbours haunted him, bestowing upon him a moral compass for the advocacy he would later champion. While roaming around the borough of Queens, he observed from the ground the creativity and hard work of people carrying heavy bundles of civilisation with them. Within this vibrant landscape, Mamdani learnt the essential virtues of social life: tolerance, unity, and the strength of collective action. His early years were a practical demonstration of the fact that the lines of civilisation were simply imaginary, and human beings were one family. This awakening was the beginning of a lifelong commitment to erasing the lines of division and empowering the silenced people. In every endeavour, he invoked the unbreakable bonds of his immigrant ancestry.

Influence of Families: Comparing Parenting Styles and Expectations

AOC's and Donald Trump's lives took different paths, largely due to their family surroundings. In Donald's case, he absorbed the worldview and aspirations of his father, Fred Trump, a well-known real estate developer. This exposure from a young age to the real estate business made Trump a born entrepreneur, a deal-maker, and a staunch capitalist. AOC had quite the opposite. She recalls her immigrant parents as having to fight hard to succeed in America, and it was this background that provided the ground for her formative years. Their struggles deeply impacted her, leading her to develop a strong sense of social justice.

The parental expectations had equally important functions in forging their attitudes towards personal and communal success. While Fred Trump wanted his son to run the family business and equate success with the money he/she would accumulate, AOC's parents wanted her to value learning, volunteerism, and serving the oppressed. These two sets of expectations helped justify their different views on wealth, privilege, and the government's role in social injustice.

In addition, the family's transmitted cultural and social attitudes made a major impact on Trump and AOC's views on immigration and inclusivity. The heavy dose of privilege associated with Trump, combined with deep roots in America, made him immigration exclusionary and 'America First' focused. AOC's family story of hardship and unifying struggle, on the other hand, made her a strong proponent of immigrants and compassion in immigration policy.

These two figures have taken strikingly different paths, which demonstrates the deep roots of family values in shaping the sociopolitical views and character of each individual.

Education Paths: Elite Schooling versus Public Institutions

The resources and opportunities available to each person in

their upbringing caused the difference in the life paths of Trump and Mohamed Mamdani. For Trump, the schooling life started at the Kew-Forest School located in Forest Hills, Queens. He went on to study at the Kew-Forest School from kindergarten until the seventh grade. Thereafter, he moved into the New York Military Academy to complete his secondary education. All this schooling, at that level, provided him direct access to a network of wealthy families abundant in social and educational resources beyond his Kew-Forest School. The experience made him slip into an understanding of what it meant to be entitled and successful at such a young age.

Mamdani, on the other hand, went through the public schooling system. This schooling, available to the economically poorer classes and often immigrants, is located in what were termed 'ethnically mixed areas' in Queens, which had their own plethora of disadvantages and advantages. His early schooling years were spent in a school system that was much poorer and economically diverse, culturally and educationally, and had to deal with social issues instead of conflicts. This made him develop an understanding of the struggle and the equity imbalance in society. He was able to see the failures in what was termed a public schooling system and the inadequate provisions that were supposed to be ideal for society's growth. The knowledge acquisition of both Trump and Mamdani warrants Trump's educational privileges considering the social and cultural factors both of them navigate. It highlights the consequences of their circumstances. Moreover, the educational experiences of Trump and Mamdani serve as the foundation to examine the sociological phenomena, shedding light on the unresolved domains in the American education system.

Examining individual worldviews of value and aspirations highlights the interdependent relationship between the occurrence of world and value systems in children from early ages and their educational exposure. The Trump and Mamdani phenomenon raises critical considerations of the degree to which dominant social policy frameworks embody inequity and the extent to which these social policy frameworks systematise these inequities.

Early Social Circles: Encounters with Diversity and Privilege

While the two men were getting to know Queens for the very first time—one of the first places they ever spent time in—they were both fortunate to witness for the first time the wide array of cultures and varying social and economic situations that were present in that area. Trump grew up in a neighbourhood filled with other wealthy individuals, and this was also true when it came to the schools that he attended. Because the schools were private, Trump always had people of the same social status around him. In this case, this was the privilege of attending a private school. This pool of schoolmates, employees and scholars was in many cases unreasonably esteemed and definitively underestimated in terms of their social means. This is because in this environment privilege was unquestioned and had nothing comparable to be juxtaposed with. On the contrary, in the basement where Mamdani spent his time, there were boys and girls from different social and economic backgrounds. In this setting, he was also with other boys and girls who were part of the economy's rosy spectacle of the time. This created a basis for a deeper social integration that was formed more from the economic and political paradigm of the time. Such social constructions were undermined and could not escape the mundane inequalities of race and class that underpinned the surrounding economies. The early years of the boys in Queens would help to shape their interactions with race and class in their later years. Because Trump was exposed to such limited social diversity, he had a fairly narrow perception of the other struggles that people from other countries faced. This was not true for Mamdani, as it is clear that his dealings with people from different countries gave him the understanding that he needed about the inequalities.

The differences between these two accounts do not distinguish the two corresponding accounts of one's privileges and the impact these privileges have on the chances and outcomes of one's life. These early social circles were the first environments in which the foundational cognitions were formed and prepared the individuals for their different pursuits, which ultimately determined the nature and extent of their success and influence.

Childhood Ambitions: Initial Career Aspirations and Role Models

The two men came from different backgrounds and grew up in the borough's surroundings, having lived in one of the most prominent and commercially developed neighbourhoods of Queens. Brought up in a family where the father was a property developer, Trump attributes his ambitions to start in the real estate industry to his father's position. With a desire and goal to add more value to the family's business, Trump was surrounded by an entrepreneurial family and had access to finances. On the other hand, in his immigrant community, Mamdani was motivated by the rebuilding spirit of community workers and their advocacy. With an undying passion for social justice and empowerment for his community, Mamdani was the one who advanced the most among these immigrants. In addition to this, Mamdani's immigrant parents were the ones who raised him to be a compassionate, equitable person with solidarity.

In addition, the societal stories as well as the dominant figures within the neighbourhoods of the participants noticeably shaped their professional goals. As Trump enjoyed the dazzle of high society and the powerful of Manhattan, Mamdani was surrounded by the tales of the common folk and their struggles with the systems. It was this contrast of experiences that drove the two of them to form different ideas of success and impact. Trump's 'role models' captured the peak of wealth and power, while Mamdani's formative figures were the brave, self-sacrificing, grassroots warriors of advocacy.

Out of these different experiences, both men constructed different stories of their youth. Nostalgia for the lost real estate empire his family had constructed motivated Trump to devote himself to expanding their family business, just as his 'role models' burnt, while Mamdani imagined himself a community organiser and advocate seeking to defend the silenced and sidelined. There is no doubt that the two spent their childhood differently – what is unquestionable is the fact that these dreams of childhood shaped the ideas and goals the two carried to their adulthood, the ideas and goals that determined their professional lives. This illustrates the powerful reality of aspirations and role models and their impact on the outlooks and decisions employed in life.

Neighbourhood Narratives: Stories from a Borough of Contrasts

One of the most ethnically diverse places on earth, Queens, was equally home to Donald Trump and Mohammed Mamdani during their formative years. The borough was a mosaic of disparate cultures, traditions and economic activities, and that, more than anything else, became the foundation of their differing world views, which was certainly a case of juxtaposition.

Queens of Trump's childhood was the epicentre of suburban riches, filled with the most expensive areas of Jamaica Estates, and was very unlike upper-middle-class New York City. Unlike the aspirations and dreams that came along with the delight of frolicking in the upper reaches of the city, Trump's narrative as a child, one filled with triumph and prosperity, was drenched head to toe in the success of the rest of America. Dominated by the spurious notion of the golden chair, his neighbourhood's rusty gates around its periphery encapsulated the reality on the other side, which was stark and rudimentary, more than one could imagine.

In contrast, for Mamdani, the Queens neighbourhood painted a very different picture. His childhood was spent in a community encased within the grips of economic dire straits and social injustices. He emphasises and celebrates adversity and the resilience that accompanies it. For Mamdani,

Queens is the very heart of the struggle and the triumph that embodies both the complexities and contradictions of the immigrant experience in America. Within this cacophonic constellation of streets and cultures, he was introduced to the high lessons of struggle, unity, and the encompassing foundations of social assault.

The borough, for instance, presented a contradictory beautiful piece of high and low. Like the gated communities in the borough that dotted the landscape and the crowded working-class tenements, there was a rich immersion in the Queens tapestry that was more than the surface of what formed the Queens experience. This experience would deeply influence the developing mental model of both Mamdani and Trump.

The time spent in Queens particularly witnessed the intersection of the two sides of the American Dream, along with the economic disappointment. Through the diverse Queens neighbourhoods, they grappled with concepts of capitalism and misery, nurturing an ideological framework that would underpin their commitment to activism. The tales woven into the geometry of Queens would echo vigorously in the actions they would take, outlining two colliding destinies rooted in the contrasting tapestries of their borough.

Economic Disparities: Witnessing Wealth Distributions Firsthand

Mamdani and Trump, just like any other boy who grew up in Queens, had an opportunity to learn about balance and opportunity, including prizes in most parts of any city as well as the disparities and other not-so-pleasing parts of any town. Their childhood and formative period was characterised in part by the unheard-of and unimaginable fortunes in other places of the city as adjacent to one who was economically challenged. One of the most important members of the family was involved in real estate, and as such, Trump was born in such golden circumstances that he had no option but to live in the city of Queens through the Trump family and had inherited the family's real estate and other associated businesses. They painted a completely different picture and, in most cases, and still, used the neck and the beat, and Mamdani was able to see the real-life struggle of the skeleton and the never-ending stories of the arms and the rest of the body in the Pachabi of the bottom of every unsolved and insightful blues. With the brightness and the shadow, which were all so decently contrasting colours of the picture and fabric of the context, as they so vibrantly live, the touch of each side of the economy was able to see the structure of the country. In the country, and when in the starting will be and still be every time, the first thing that a boy witnesses is the city. This is what is depicted in the contrasting places.

Not only did these differing experiences impact their distinct goals and ambitions, but they also acted as the crucible in which their core beliefs on the uses and abuses of wealth and income inequality in society were forged. The economic consequences of the people's lives they witnessed and their own lived experiences shaped the basis of their policies and the advocacy work which they continue to push. This continues to remain as a testimony to how these differing socio-economic encounters influenced them from an early stage of their lives.

Conflicts as Formative Aspects of Life: The Lesson of Adversity

In the case of the two individuals in the study, Trump and Mamdani, while in Queens, faced a number of conflicts which were vital in the formation of their attitudes and theories regarding conflict and the case of adversity. For Trump, the problems were conflict with relation to a certain level of competition, as well as social standing. The case of Trump was born with a silver spoon as the child of a rich real estate developer and faced a lot of anxiety regarding maintaining and surpassing what his family was achieving economically. His conflicts were a cause of the painful pressures that accompany living in an economically affluent family; his response was to develop a striving and aggressive approach to achieving personal success. This primary conflict of holding wealth and power was what focused and developed the later view of Trump on individualistic capitalism.

On the other hand, Mamdani's formative conflicts were tied to issues of migration, bigotry, and poverty. As an immigrant to the United States, he arrived in Queens from Uganda and suffered from discrimination and biases that profoundly impacted his worldview in his formative years. These challenges gave him an appreciation for defending the oppressed from the systemic plight. His conflicts instilled in him a recognition of the need for social change, which became the basis for his advocacy and community organising work.

These two individuals and their subjects of focus illustrate the micro dimension of conflict and the macro dimension of the underlying ideology. In contrast to Mamdani, who was discriminated against and observed the inequities of society, Trump had encounters with discrimination and social inequities that ignited in him a passion for social justice and equity, motivating him to work for the equity and justice of all.

Both of these individuals demonstrate the critical nature of formative conflict and ideology in conflict. In other words, their early years and the life events they experienced shaped their ideology and set the policy direction for their adult lives. Understanding these formative conflicts sheds some light on their diverse approaches to governance, privilege, and the American Dream.

2
Defining Success
Trump's Business Empire Versus Mamdani's Community Organising

Historical Context of Success

Success is a part of American culture, but its definition has changed and is rooted in capitalism. Over the years, it has influenced and transformed the relentless lifestyle of Americans, in which the dream motivated the pursuit of wealth through hard work and sacrifice. From the early settlers to the industrial revolution, success has been inextricably linked to the value of capitalism. The country's transition from agriculture to industry opened up new opportunities for success, primarily through entrepreneurial zeal and wealth.

Embracing the American dream attracted financially and socially reputable individuals to the concept. Being part of the American dream required endorsing that concept. People believed the vision's reward would manifest when they received assurances that their hard work and dreams would soon come true. This backdrop explains the timeline in which Americans inextricably linked success to their wealth and disdain for capitalism. In addition, the emergence of consumer culture alongside the development of media during the last century cultivated the desire-born images of success defined by consumption and wealth. However, despite their triumphal appearance, the narratives of success consistently featured stark inequalities and obstacles to achieving it. These developments further complicated the ever-present intersection between capitalism and social inequities. In the present era, the parameters of success are still defined by the phenomenon of global capitalism, with its attendant breakneck technology, globalisation, and shifting patterns of employment. So, in modern capitalism, success is defined not only by money but also by the ability to innovate, adapt, and endure. Understanding the historical evolution and interconnectedness of success with capitalism provides insightful knowledge of the manner in which these symbiotic constructs have sculpted social order, individual ambitions, and the economy as a whole.

Trump's Business Philosophy

The business traits that define Donald Trump are ambition, calculated risk, success, and an attempt on all fronts to achieve it. Born into a family with an already successful real estate empire, Trump learnt what "business" was all about in his early years. During his time at his father's company, he acquired knowledge and skills in real estate development and property management. When he went to do business on his own, he concentrated on high-end luxurious real estate properties, branding them to be worth even more than what they were actually offered at. The Trump Organization centred on increase and expansion, even if it was at the cost of 'opulence'. They borrowed heavily to acquire luxurious properties. Despite encountering both failures and successes, they grew accustomed to the 'Trump Trap.' Business was business, and every business risk, regardless of the number, was a bold and noble attempt. The real major business Trump ended up in was 'real' business, a form of entertainment taken to the level of every real estate tycoon in the US at the time – Trump's branding he rightly owned and staunchly defended. Few Trump-brand hotels were built alongside investments in every real estate 'palace'. The case was that Trump's branding, when combined with controlled media, was sharp and powerful. Whether people loved or hated it, many in the world viewed Trump as the embodiment of the 'American Dream'. While many businesses suffered greatly, Trump's supporters became more energised, pursuing both fame and profit, igniting passion amidst fierce competition. Trump's business philosophy stated that dollars are what matter, while everything else requires the cover of smoke. Anything else is the rest.

This analysis has defended capitalism and claimed that competition and personal economic gain were the cornerstones of American capitalism. This, in turn, placed Trump as the embodiment of the American self-made businessman. This chapter seeks to unpack the ways in which Trump's business dealings reflect American capitalism and the issues it raises pertaining to culture, infrastructure, and success.

Economic Ambition and Real Estate

Let's consider real estate as one avenue of economic ambition, exemplified by Donald Trump's business empire. He entered the real estate industry with a vision of extravagance that he later brought to life in Trump Tower and other lofty projects. These constructions Trump undertook represent his sheer desire to gain wealth and power and are reflective of the drive to take over the real estate industry. Not only did he want to gain riches beyond imagination, but he also wanted to dominate over other developers. His self-image as a wealthy capitalist infused the business he promoted and all its dealings with luxury and material gain. His actions were driven by a desire for acceptance in the business sector, reflecting an intense ambition to achieve success. Such is the power of his actions and reputation.

Mamdani's perspective is a nuanced break from the predominant narrative, as he highlights the powerful transformative impact real estate can have on communities. Instead of referring to real estate as a tool for individual enrichment, Mamdani advocates for a model that puts marginalised communities at the centre and promotes the idea that housing is a fundamental human right. His treatment of real estate is premised on social justice and the right to adequate housing, and it serves as a critique of the prevailing notion of economic success in this area. By arguing that real estate can serve to lift the disadvantaged, Mamdani broadens the understanding of success in property development, shifting the focus to integrated community wellness and prosperity.

Additionally, analysing these contrasting viewpoints emphasises the complexity of real estate valuation as an expression of personal and social concern. It epitomises the clash between the vaulting real estate vision of Trump and the community-orientated activism of Mamdani. It highlights the growing divide between differing visions and the extent of economic ambition and activism. Real estate, in its intricate technical and social dimensions, reflects a discourse on the nature of success and the purpose of responsibility in the generation of wealth. In this regard, the discussion of ambition in real estate sheds light on the different value systems that are able to shape the core of American capitalism and, in so doing, refreshes the discourse on the nature of prosperity and the responsibility that comes with the pursuit of wealth.

Personal branding is a measure of triumph

While carrying out business and community leadership activities, the role of personal branding is crucial when it comes to public image and influence. In the case of Donald Trump, personal branding is an achievement, and it comes as no surprise how much it is enmeshed within his business empire. Through marketing and image reinvention of his name as a marker of prosperity, Trump has associated his name with opulence, wealth, and power, something which he has skilfully cultivated over the years. This branding is not only limited to his real estate business but also extends to a myriad of other business activities, his political career, commercial enterprises, and media presence. As for the Trump brand, it is not only the label of his properties but also an intangible asset, which signifies a certain lifestyle and status for the owners. With great ease, the Trump name has been associated with prosperity, and it is of great importance to highlight that this recognition has been the outcome of a deliberate strategy designed to put him in the public eye. In America, Trump's self-promotion and marketing have, in fact, managed to elevate his personal brand to a heralded accomplishment, a testament to his claim of holding the American Dream. In stark contrast, within community organisations, personal branding is quite different. In the case of Mamdani, it is not about self-glory but selfless and collective empowerment.

Instead of curating a personal brand, Mamdani invests his energies in the importance of identity and the silent voices of the marginalised. Mamdani employs a strategy that focuses on building trust, fostering social cohesion, and telling the stories of the marginalised in the narrative. For Mamdani, the yardstick of his success is the change he brings about in the lives of the people and the communities he serves, and not the accolades or the riches he accumulates. While Mamdani is selfless in his disdain for self-promotion and works for the community's uplifting, he provides a much-needed fresh view on leadership and success, defined by compassion and communal growth. The difference in approach to personal branding is stark also between Mamdani and Trump. While Trump epitomises individualism by seeking the spotlight and financial gains, Mamdani is motivated by a sense of community, which represents a completely opposite and more empathetic approach. These examples make the more distilled arguments about capitalism and values in America more illuminating.

Mamdani's Community-Focused Success

Mamdani's approach to defining success emphasises community focus and welfare, contrasting sharply with Trump's business empire, which prioritises individual gains and profits. While the average business owner is more concerned about acquiring wealth on a personal level, Mamdani is more concerned about the development of marginalised societies. He shifts his focus from individuals to the larger society, observing that success cannot be achieved individually; rather, it must be earned collectively by the entire community. This foundation reflects his commitment to democracy and the central principles of participatory and inclusive decision-making.

Mamdani's success in forming theory revolves around success in community organising. He works with and supports diverse groups during his advocacy on behalf of tenants, immigrants, and other neglected people. Mamdani helps people to create their own community and provides means for people to help themselves to lead a life, which is a right for people. This is referred to as social justice, as Mamdani believes success is what helps communities to grow.

An essential aspect of Mamdani's framework is considering social metrics that go beyond the bottom line. He argues that success should be measured by the measurable gains in the improvement of life, access to education and preventive healthcare, and the welfare of marginalised populations. Mamdani's social impact focus indicates that he appreciates the structural issues that affect marginalised people and the need for change on the ground.

Furthermore, Mamdani's focus on the community asserts the need to build lasting, mutually beneficial relations within the community and the surrounding areas. He advocates for the inclusion of members of the community and other stakeholders in the decision-making process and mobilises them to take charge. This model of success which Mamdani advocates for encourages collective action and ownership. This model of action shifts the frame of reference for success, and in so doing, it offers a new outlook on prosperity, which is predicated on the advancement of integrated societies.

In conclusion, we conclude that redefining success to focus on community well-being, the availability of opportunities, and participatory governance—as described in Mamdani's case study—remains valid and gains even greater relevance in the current context. This paradigm of Mamdani illustrates the importance of empowerment and inclusive development at the grassroots level. It also highlights the importance of development for those who have been uplifted. As the measurement of success continues to evolve, Mamdani serves as a reminder that the goals of success must shift according to his argument. It should, and must, include the aspirations of the people from whom new definitions of success and progress are being derived.

Social Metrics and Community Impact

Equity and justice are new frontiers for an entrepreneurial and outcome-orientated approach to funding social projects. As Mamdani demonstrates, an approach to social funding which emphasises social metrics encourages social entrepreneurs to develop social finance business models which embrace positive community change. Measuring social impact pivots funding layers to replenish community social infrastructure. Balanced, simultaneously sustaining ecosystems underscore this approach.

In Mamdani's approach, community impact is not simply understood in transactional and financial terms. The impact is gauged by how the people going about their daily activities socially experience life. It requires measuring social capital, social inclusion, social services provisioning, and social quality of life. Focusing on social policy outcomes, equity is not only about equal opportunity policy but also about equal outcome policy. It is aimed at broader, enduring social change by lifting people's voices and addressing the persistent inequities in the social fabric.

Clearly, the focus of social impact funding also includes the community on which economic activities are performed. Mamdani's focused capitalism examines the community and the externals of capitalistic activities, enquiring into the community's and ecology's enduring impacts. To this end, equity and justice are ultimate purposes of Mamdani's capitalism – the more social impacts that are generated, the more capitalist the system is.

Echoing the practices of advocates of degrowth, Mamdani reframes success by incorporating and valuing community impact as the most important measure of success. This redefinition helps expand the discourse on success by shifting the focus to achieving success in a socially responsible, balanced, and corporately sustainable manner.

Mamdani's approach emphasises the importance of social metrics and community impact, advocating for a shift in the definition of prosperity to be anchored on the human dimensions of it. This shift in definition reflects a change in the prevailing social attitudes and norms about achievement to a more caring and compassionate framework. By doing this, Mamdani takes the conversation about success beyond the attainment of wealth and material goods by advocating for the inclusion of dignity, social cohesion, and community welfare in the definition.

Contrasting Measurements: Wealth vs. Well-being

When analysing the relationship between wealth and well-being, it highlights the complex issues surrounding the reasons for and focus of a society's progress. On the one hand, wealth and material affluence, the usual parameters of success, are, on the contrary, counter-argued to be the holistic welfare of people and society. This paradigm difference explains the differing approaches of businessman Donald Trump and the community organiser Mamdani, each representing different views on what progress and wealth mean. From Trump's perspective, capitalist in nature, the industrialist, as do the rest of the capitalists, believes in one bottom line profit: to make as much money as one can accumulate and own in the form of real estate, companies, and assets. In paradoxical reasoning, this capitalist mentality believes profit margin, the stock market, and GDP growth are the only measures of the wealth of a country, to even be considered heretical to the country's welfare. From this perspective, Mamdani's argument focuses on social well-being and expands the notion of wealth to something more all-embracing and wealth-creating that transcends the shackles of the economy. Civic solidarity, community resource accessibility, and resources and opportunities that enable every individual to partake in the society and economy of the country are inclusive and reiterative. Prosperity in this regard is synonymous with the community. It is in the health, education, and humanity of the people and society at large that true wealth lies, not in the monetary illusion.

The dual approaches hinge on the question of whether capitalism ought to pursue profit unthinkingly or whether it can be turned to the service of the common good. Such rifts are felt acutely in the American socio-economy, where the question of profit and advancement rests entirely on the individual in opposition to more social, human-centered advancement. At the same time, it makes necessary the critique of the damages of wealth-only policies. In particular, these could be widening societal inequalities, degradation of the environment, and the weakening of social ties. In this case, the debate on wealth and well-being can serve as a starting point for analysing the foundational values of American capitalism with a view to its other, more socially constructive models.

Philosophical Underpinnings of Capitalism

Philosophically, capitalism is a complex combination of notions that serves as a socio-economic system. Individual freedom and self-interest, as the primary drivers of capitalism, prove the philosophy of freedom. Individualism, as a philosophy, regards a person's capability to take control of their lives and be successful as a form of achievement. The advocacy of competition as well as the ability of the market to resource the economy strives for its liberal philosophy domestically. The primary principle of these capitalist economies, private property, is a reflection of the natural law right of owning and ruling one's own possessions profoundly posed by Locke. This philosophy states that there is no limit to the wealth a person can gain, and consequently, the limit in a market economy is the wealth that society can opt to distribute. The self-interested nature of a person is a driving force in a society, and thus, the overall well-being of the society is maximised. This is the principle of the overall utility capitalist model of society. The consequence of these models shapes their critique of one society's philosophy of non-market, advocating for socialist models of society, with

Marxists critiquing the capitalist models.

Profound critiques have been directed at capitalism's focus on profitability, particularly regarding how the commodification of labour leads to inequalities, alienation, and exploitation. The mere transactions of relationships for a Kantian cause are an issue, while a Rawlian would be more concerned with the disproportionate wealth and lack of opportunity as an affront to their concept of justice. Such philosophy is taken to question the capitalistic society and to what extent it serves the civilisational values. Moreover, the effect of capitalism on the environment has sparked ethical questions about contemporary capitalism's sustainability and justice for future generations, thus reaching farther than the conventional capitalistic focus. Whenever capitalism is discussed in the context of divergent capitalist success definitions, the lack of a philosophy that describes the contrasting value systems and frameworks of success is astounding. They help clarify the ideological questions surrounding economic policies, wealth distribution, and national debates. The lack of philosophy, which describes the contrasting value systems and frameworks of success, is astounding. These assist in clarifying the ideological questions regarding the economic policies, wealth policies, and the general state of the country debates. Definitions of success in capitalism encompass various frameworks and would undoubtedly foster engaging discussions about the philosophy of economic success. The debates revolving around wealth policies and the state of the country discuss the overall condition of deeply interwoven argumentative veins.

Influence of Personal Backgrounds

No one can deny the influence of personal backgrounds on people's philosophies and notions of success. Whether it is Trump orZohran Mamdani, the repercussions of their formative years have influenced their understandings of achievement, privilege, and the American capitalist system. For instance, Trump was born into a wealthy family and grew up surrounded by his father's real estate empire. From an early age, Trump was taught that financial success and material wealth equate to achievement. His surroundings during the formative years were filled with wealth; thus, there was a competitive, individualistic approach where validation was based on the wealth and power a person possesses. Zohran Mamdani, an immigrant child, grew up with a strong sense of community and engaged in social justice activism. Living in New York City as an immigrant, Mamdani was able to see the realities of the underprivileged and the inequality that is created by capitalism. His involvement in community-based organisations at an early age made him believe in the importance of social cohesion and collective well-being.

Also, Mamdani's integrative scholarship and activism in both Africa and the United States have refined his focus on the globe's social and economic interrelations. These different lived experiences have shaped, in confounding manners, Trump's and Mamdani's worldviews and how they choose to approach the notion of success. For Trump, personal advancement and acquisition of tangible assets are the primary goals of success. In contrast, the experiences of Mamdani, primarily economic in Africa, have led him to the notion of success as the ability to uplift the entire community and have resources available to all. These personal stories, defined by the stout social class, culture, and position, are instrumental in forming the political ideas of the prominent personalities and, thus, must be taken into consideration. The personal stories of Trump and Mamdani make clearer the rationale behind their definitions of success and their role in the broader context of American capitalism.

Pondering American Principles

In pondering the two contrasting paths that Trump and Mamdani have taken in their definitions of success and how they measure achievement, it is necessary to reflect on their relevance to American ideals. The founding principles of equality and opportunity and the varying interpretations of the American Dream – it's clear that the divided approaches of the two are the very epitome of the complexity that American society is made of. To Trump, success is in the accumulation of wealth and the construction of a personal brand, and it is in this assertion that the logic of the self-made capitalist and the boundless American policies is ascribed. The epitome of capitalist enterprise, it is in the very notion of success that is most admired within the American psyche and is synonymous with Trump's Empire. On the contrary, it is in the alternative formulation that Mamdani's social justice advocacy and community organising portray that American ideals are constructed. Unlike Trump's model of success, where the aim is primarily self-serving, his model fosters the notion that success is in the advancement of social justice. This contrast, this contradiction, this divergence in narrative is necessary for what is to be called the American success story. Of American capitalism and social progress, the values are easily taken for granted, and as a result, this idea of success is reflective upon the capitalist notion of wealth, where the boundaries of community-orientated effort are questioned.

Moreover, as we address inequality, oppression, and poverty, the difference between Trump's corporate empire and Mamdani's activism reveals unresolved contradictions within American society. These contradictions force us to rethink the fundamental ideas of democracy and liberty and pay closer attention to the nation's conscience. In the end, the contrast between Trump's and Mamdani's definitions of success is a striking illustration of the complexity of American values. It is a call to rethink the essential attributes of American identity and where the country stands with its achievement, wealth, and social welfare. In doing so, we might pave the way toward a new American Dream, one that offers a more expansive and egalitarian vision with various forms of success and the enrichment of every citizen.

3
The Housing Crisis
Competing Visions For America's Housing Emergency

Overview of America's Housing Challenge

In the United States, the housing sector is at a critical point that is historically and currently complex. These challenges are deeply rooted and multifaceted. In order to grasp the condition of our nation's housing segment, it is necessary to grapple with the past that gave birth to the current scenario. When considering the Depression and the housing policies that were implemented after the Second World War, there is a foundation that has shaped the American housing sector. There was Suburbia, which was promoted by government policies that also resulted in single-family homeownership while urban housing was ignored.

There was also the Fair Housing Act of 1968, which, along with other subsidised housing programs, sought to address structural inequalities that still dominate the framework of our society. However, these efforts still did not close the gap in mortgage credit, housing of diminished quality, and homeownership. Turning to the current context, the impacts of the housing market crash in 2008 are still visible, along with the mortgage foreclosure crisis, particularly affecting the underprivileged population. Housing insecurity, especially for low-income households, has become a reality.

The soaring cost of housing, which has resulted from the lack of correlation between wages and housing prices, and the frantic addition of overpriced housing at the cost of dilapidated and abandoned buildings, greatly supports the legacy of affluent fusion developments, alongside the acute lack of affordable housing, compounded by the COVID-19 pandemic and the surge of gentrification. These and similar developments have neglected the society of renters, low-wage families, and individuals who already lack proper housing. They have doubly marginalised these individuals.

This right to housing is fundamental, and along with co-existing inequities spanning from the past to the present, which have held and restricted people to some of the deepest tribulations, has put America at a crossroads of decisions to be made. These decisions need to embrace historical inequities, where housing is a basic human need, alongside the modern-day challenges that America is currently facing. They should integrate inclusive approaches to policymaking with struggles related to land use, zoning control, financing, and the lack of commitment to stable housing access needs. To make these policies effective, systemic cross-relations between America's socio-economics and housing policies need to be considered.

Economic Frameworks: Luxury Development and Deregulation

Deregulation and luxury development have become the guiding principles of the American housing debate. Advocates of luxury development posit that the construction of upscale housing tailored specifically for a particular region enables the region in question to achieve urban renewal, achieve economic development, and attract new investments. It becomes a point of contention when the free market is called upon, particularly to defend luxury housing, by suggesting that there is a market for such properties because there is a sizable segment of the population willing to purchase them. Deregulation, as a process that is connected to the construction of such properties, seeks to reduce the inquiry and construction processes by removing development deemed unnecessary. The assumption is that, to the extent that the existing social restrictions and the subsequent development of the rational market disconnect, there is a reduced likelihood that social restrictions will influence the rational development of the market and, in the event that they do, the housing costs vis-a-vis the offer will have reasonably low prices. This contention hinges on the assertion that the individual choices offered and the low-furnished solutions are linked here, whereas there are claims that luxury housing development is a solution to economic problems of the society. It is those who oppose the development of such housing who argue that the development of such housing is a negative development socially and economically in the movement of the lower strata of society, who are being gentrified out and being replaced by lower- and sub-middle-class families. The so-called 'luxury overbuilding' is a shortage of social housing that ends the conversation on social and economic diversity at the neighbourhood scale. This critique provides a glimpse into the wider community as a social unit, social connection and social ecology influenced by the construction of luxury housing.

More importantly, the distribution of these luxury units remains a matter of concern for urban equity because it is inaccessible to a large part of the population. At the same time, the other side of the deregulation debate is charged with neglecting safety, the environment, and planning for the future in favour of short-term profits. The discussions on luxury development and deregulation, on the other hand, evoke extreme and opposing views on the place of the market in housing and the community-developer relationship. As these discussions grow, the need to understand luxury and affordability, urban trade-offs, and what that does to the inclusiveness and sustainability of our cities becomes instrumental.

The Impact of Public Policy on Housing Markets

Public policy is of great importance to defining and affecting the rest of the market. It determines accessibility and affordability and the amount and quality of housing stock. The zoning and land use policy combined with the subsidies and tax policies can tilt the entire housing balance. To understand the crisis and the needed reforms, one can examine the historical evolution of housing policy in the US. Pay particular attention to how the policy geography of a country determines resource and opportunity distribution. It is critical to social equity to have affordable housing, fair housing, and anti-discrimination policies. Advocacy resource allocation is most effective in improving the socio-economic status of many people. The same goes for public-private partnerships and housing relief programmes. The legal regime dealing with the building and housing safety standards and the legal regime dealing with the health and security of inhabitants are vital. In a housing policy, macroeconomic and finance policies dealing with the economy in the social rest of the economy are equally vital. Public policy in the rest of the economy is vital.

For effect, policies targeted towards monetary expansion,

given the central bank policies, can influence the economic availability of credit to homebuyers and the stability of the real estate market. Fiscal policies, such as the architecture of property taxation, coupled with direct budgetary subsidies to housing, influence the economic benefits of owning a home as well as the benefits of investing in real estate. Moreover, policies on the urban environment as well as transport have a bearing on the accessibility of housing and urban expansion. In the midst of these, the convergence of some element of public policy with the housing market and the real estate market shows that the policies made can have deep-seated consequences on people, families, and society at large. A deeper understanding of these policy frameworks is important to ensure that the housing policies made are sustainable and equitable to the many members of society. The analysis of the policies should be complemented by the attempt to imagine and the desire to design new housing policies that aim to an inclusive housing systems that foster resilience and prosperity for all.

Social Housing: The Case for Tenant Rights and Protections

Social housing has always been associated with fair living standards and appropriate accommodation for every individual. With social housing, tenant rights and protections are indeed the most important elements in the perpetual fight for housing justice. Understanding the social housing issue sheds light on the narrative of protecting tenant rights and the housing system protections.

Social housing aims at going beyond the provision of shelter to offer inclusive and stable living environments for residents with all the necessary empowerment. The approach to tenant rights defends the dignity of all people, offering security and the building of strong, integrated neighbourhoods across cities. The argument is premised on the notion that every individual and family must access safe, decent, and affordable housing. Societies must ensure that this is the most important step towards ensuring social and economic prosperity.

Tenant protections must address the inequities of power between landlords and tenants, where tenants face exploitation, discrimination, and even the threat of homelessness. This requires specific laws addressing one of the most important aspects of human life, housing, which includes the affirmation of adequate housing, non-discriminatory leasing procedures, anti-retaliation policies, and the right to remedies in housing violation cases. In addition, robust community resilience and a stable housing market are core to the market, including rent control, barriers to eviction, and the right to direct collective negotiation.

Counselling centres are not the only option we have for self-care, and creating a positive environment in the community is also a positive step towards a healthy holistic life. There are also many positive civic contributions—giving them a resolve to remove inequity begins to break down the silos. Additionally, focused social housing attempts to remove disparity and build communities upwards, removing inequity barriers while widening the support of society.

At the core of the advocacy for tenant rights is the need for community engagement and participatory processes, where residents are decision-makers over the policies that affect their housing to foster a culture of agency, accountability, and togetherness in the neighbourhood. This ethos links with the idea that housing is not only a commodity but a human necessity, the fulfilment of which enables the thriving of a community and the nurturing of prosperity in common.

Impacts on communities: Testimonies from the neighbourhoods of New York

Deep in the borough of Brooklyn, surrounded by strong artistic and cultural diversity, we come face to face with the impacts of housing policies on the day-to-day activities of New Yorkers. Consider the story of the Ramirez family, which has lived in their rent-stabilised apartment for many decades. Because of the recent rush of luxury developments, they are finding their rent increasing dramatically, making it increasingly difficult for them to continue living in their residence. The social dislocation they are facing is troubling, in that all of the social ties, community support systems, and the concept of belonging are all disappearing.

In the Bronx, the public housing tenants articulate their anger about the ongoing neglect and disinvestment in their living conditions. While market-driven policies ignore their plight, families live with the disintegration of fundamental infrastructure, pervasive unserviced spaces, and a general feeling of abandonment. These stories highlight the actual human cost from contending housing policies, denying the inequity of housing and the opportunities that derive from inequitable policies.

In Queens, we find another dimension to the housing crisis. Here, we observe the vitality of flourishing immigrant communities situated within the processes of gentrification and wage stagnation. The ever-increasing collection of immigrant families, to whom affordable housing is fundamental to their aspiration for social stability and upward mobility, find themselves in the onslaught of luxury condominiums and higher-end gentrified developments. Caught between the dilemma of cultural preservation and economic advancement, families become increasingly visible within a silenced grid of contending perceptions of the city.

The boroughs have a multitude of communities with a myriad of stories which highlight how deeply housing policies can affect the structure of a community. Each story showcases the intertwining of housing with profound issues of socio-economic inequity, systemic racism, and the notion of community, stressing the importance of housing not as a mere shelter, but as a fundamental element of dignity and identity, both personal and collective. The narratives outlined above prompt a reflection on the implications of housing policies on the people who inhabit New York City as well as the policies themselves, especially the underlying philosophies on which the policies are grounded.

Regulatory Environments: Local versus Federal Influence

The local and national economic and regulatory policies of the zones underscore the profound impact of local and federal policies on the ongoing housing crisis. At the local level, the regulatory policies that govern the types of construction that may be undertaken, as well as their geographic density and the allocation of resources for affordable housing within the region, impact the housing stock and affordability. All cities and towns are empowered to develop zoning and building regulatory frameworks that address local construction and housing market concerns. Such policies may, however, lead to imbalances in housing urbanism and in building construction within a neighbourhood, thus aggravating the affordable housing and housing urbanism problems. Federal policies on housing, on the other hand, operate as a collection of unsynchronised policies bordering on the federal housing programme and its various funding sources. Such policies are implemented by the HUD and FHFA, and their resultant housing policies operate nationally.

Affordable housing subsidies and mortgage insurance policies, along with the regulation of financial institutions and the housing market, fall under the broad range of Federal Initiatives. The balance of federal policies and local government control creates dynamic tension because federal policies slice through local regulatory systems, often leading to irregularities and complications. This complex concern, along with the many policies on the housing crisis, requires a grasp of the federal and local policies that integrate when responding to the housing crisis. The responsiveness local governments demonstrate, and the needed coordinated approach at the national level, create a paradoxical approach to responding to the housing emergency. Additionally, the local governments' differences in available resources and capacities require a tailored approach that appreciates the varying situations of the local authorities. Local and federal policies are intertwined in such a way that the housing crisis can be solved only through cohesive and unsplit policies that unify local actions with national policies. Only when these policies integrate local actions can the housing crisis be resolved and minimal levels of housing, along with fostered inclusive and lively communities, be provided.

Investments and Incentives: Examining Market Dynamics

The interplay of investments and incentives that foster both development and housing affordability significantly affects the housing market's dynamics. When we analyse the housing market's dynamics with respect to its root causes, it is evident that stakeholders like developers, lenders, and municipal authorities influence trends and their subsequent effects on society. We must thoroughly review these dynamics for effective policy design and implementation to address the housing crisis.

Investment decisions form the core of market dynamics. Large housing developers focus on profit opportunities and tend to construct luxury housing that, in most cases, is tailored towards high-income earners, whereas smaller housing developers tend to gauge the market and invest in housing designed for low-income earners. These investments are made on the basis of incentives that have been determined at the local and federal government levels, such as tax incentives and subsidies, as well as policies designed to influence profit and risk levels. Thus, the existing incentives determine both the types and quantities of housing units available in the market, which subsequently shape the overall housing market.

In addition, with respect to the particular context and relevance of each aspect of the market, there is a need to study the underlying causes and consequences beyond those already discussed. Tax incentives for social housing and tenant protections, for example, can allow for socially equitable development, while poorly constructed incentives for social housing can maintain development imbalance.

The housing market is also illustrative of the degree of interdependence among several sectors of the housing industry. Real estate, finance, construction, and other sectors deeply influence the market balance affected by investments and services from each industry. Finally, the state also controls the market through direct measures such as zoning policies and land use planning as well as less direct methods intended to manage private and social goals.

Grasping these intricate interactions entails an analysis of historical records, contemporaneous activities, and predictions for the future. Recognising relationships between investments, incentives, and housing markets allows policymakers and advocacy groups to develop strategies informed by practical considerations with an emphasis on housing stability, economic pluralism, and resilient communities. In the pursuit of sustainable and equitable housing for the current and future generations, we cannot afford to ignore the complexities of the market.

Case Studies: Successes and Failures in Urban Housing Solutions

To understand decisions regarding public policy and market

dynamics, where theory closely aligns with reality, one must view them through the lens of case studies on urban housing solutions. The housing crisis is a very complex issue, and only through attempts that were made and failures that were confronted can the complex constituents of the problem be well understood. Offline, there is complex infrastructure attuned to strategic public-private partnerships alongside the government and the community that can aid in achieving revitalisation in low-income localities complemented through inclusionary development policy. These public infrastructure case studies present a development story with inclusionary policy orientations that low-income locality development can be successful if there is a focus on social housing along with other social infrastructure. On the other hand, retrogressive urban renewal and regeneration cut off by gentrification and cascades of displacement phenomena are needed, alongside other devastating case studies, to help illuminate the other extreme of the spectrum, which reveals how other urban housing case studies can unmask the significant instances of replication of total inequality among those involved. These winner-loser scenarios present the case for unmasking the significant reservoirs that lie silently beneath the surface regarding housing interventions. Furthermore, the assimilation of mixed-income housing case studies from a variety of urban areas with deeply segmented socio-economic statuses provides close proximity to study the consequences and, alongside, the conflicts that arise from attempts to coalesce diverse socio-economic strata horizontally. Failures in achieving urban-scale spaces with social justice and equity also shed light on the rigid structures of the frameworks, along with the deeper underlying regulatory structures that are thin and pliable. These juxtaposed case studies furnish the knowledge that housing policies are closely tied to social justice, and complex interrelations must be managed in urban housing to satisfy democracy.

Critical Perspectives: Ideological Clash Over Housing Justice

The above paragraph serves as both an abstract and an introduction to an ideological critique to be situated around issues concerning 'housing justice'. 'Social justice', about which people have written and debated, is integral to 'distributional justice', and 'social' pertains to the provision of an undemocratic governance system within which the citizens of the country have to reside. 'Need' as a concept is instrumental in clarifying adequate governance concerning 'housing' living spaces within the geography of a given country. The answers to such broad questions have evoked a whole set of ideologies. From being more to the right of the spectrum to the left, people have provided answers regarding the role a government ought to perform, from leaving the provision of dwelling spaces to the market to how many citizens should reside within the territory of a sovereign country in the world, bordered by concrete and fences. Many individuals on the left advocate for citizens' rights, even though the entire universe should also be considered. Unquote.

Professors Michael and M. C. Hill, in their work, understand and tackle ideology within its various plural conceptions. Hill makes use of the Stanfield Report case, a mid-20th-century report from Canada, as he engages in the ideological critique and analysis of the case. *The Left* represented a significant portion of the left-of-centre political economy. 'The Left' stood for the citizens of Canada and offered the right to uncompensated assumption of the lands of the First Nations.

In this regard, the discussions surrounding housing justice serve as a glimpse into a broader conflict that profoundly impacts the fundamental nature of America. Finding a compromise between such opposing positions is undoubtedly a challenging task. To design housing reforms that are socially just and equitable, it is crucial to grasp the origins and consequences of this conflict. Only by analysing the framing narratives and assessing their actual impacts can we start to carve out avenues for dialogue and constructive action. The frame of divergent cross-case research on housing justice, along with efforts to understand policies from other countries, must also be very rigorous. To overcome the silos and narrow the differences on a just approach to the right to housing, these issues must be addressed.

Paths Forward: Bridging Visions for Sustainable Housing Reforms

At this point in the housing policy's trajectory, it is clear that the resolution will spring from some equilibrium point among the competing visions.

As demonstrated previously, the ideological battle for housing justice is a serious issue, as the fundamental strategies used to address America's housing crisis are fundamentally incompatible. However, progress now requires that a deliberate attempt be made to reconcile the differences in the perspectives.

One step in this direction is the willingness to facilitate the advocacy planks for luxury development and deregulation on the one hand, and social housing and tenant rights on the other. The idea from this engagement is that housing policies put forth in the public arena would strive to be novel, brave, and inclusive. Such approaches to the visions should be aimed at the satisfaction of the housing crisis because they appreciate and recognise the existence of contending viewpoints. It proposes a scenario where stakeholders think of the housing issue in terms of commonality and devoid of rigid ideological tussles about the core elements and the relative importance of the housing crisis.

Moreover, cross-silo visions for sustainable housing reforms require an examination of the housing system's dynamics at the level of the underlying structures. This means evaluating the regulatory system, the market, the community, and their social and equity impacts at all levels. Policy and advocacy that combine qualitative and quantitative approaches often yield the insights needed to grapple with the intricate nuances that inform the formulation and execution of multi-pronged, interventional frameworks. This, too, stands to advance the discourse of housing as a fundamental human right, moving beyond the instrumental logic of the housing market toward the ethos of human flourishing and democracy.

The forward-looking strategy has dialogue and systemic analysis as foundational elements in the continuation of the exploration of innovation in public-private and cross-sector collaboration. Additionally, there is strong public-private collaboration between governmental agencies and private sector firms, focussing on investing necessary resources, utilising required knowledge, and deploying innovation to address the sustainable housing dilemma beyond the simplistic binary of public versus private. This collaboration makes the housing ecosystem pliable, resilient, and inclusive, supported by public and private stakeholders working together towards creatively envisioned future developments that include mixed-income projects and community land trusts. It also facilitates financing that is easily accessible, promoting green aspirations for neighbourhoods shaped by the diverse dreams of the community.

In conclusion, we make the vision of housing sustainable for the future as we embark on the climb to integrate sustainable reform and housing as a basic right without the unjust spatial set. As reasoned worrying and critique of approaches deepens, and with active partnership and shared collective strategic action, the desire for housing will be fulfilled, housing will be accessible for all residing within American borders, and the phrase 'the violence is justified' will become meaningless.

4
Healthcare
Market or Right?

Historical Context and Current Landscape

More than any other nation worldwide, the USA has had to wrestle with the philosophical, political, economic, and cultural features surrounding the provision and utilisation of health care. This complex interplay has undoubtedly influenced the evolution of the USA's healthcare systems. As the 20th century ushered in, health insurance was starting to gain traction. Having the concept of health insurance in the USA was being tethered to the sponsoring employer healthcare plans. This was thus the first stepping-stone to the ongoing controversies perpetuated by capitalism in healthcare. The depression period did arguably bring to the forefront the issue of the provision of health care in the country and initiated the much-needed conversations regarding state responsibility pertaining to health care insurance. This was the era when President Franklin D. Roosevelt set forward the proposition for the introduction of a national health care system for the USA. The proposal was immense, but the realisation was less than underwhelming.

Coming onto the other side of World War II, there was a visible surge in the health insurance provided by the employer. The model sustained dominance and unrivalled status in the health insurance system of the country for multiple following decades. There was, however, a disconcerting side to the model. It was the marginalised populations and the economically deprived individuals that were the worst off. Disparity in access and coverage was a tragic and disparaging byproduct of the system. Again, a system that was supposed to do the best for the individuals sustained the worst suffering.

Disparities within the population triggered the civil rights movement, which drove advocacy for universal healthcare. It stagnated, and the question remained whether healthcare was a right or a privilege that was tied to employment and finances.

The offset of Medicare and Medicaid in 1965 was a historical turning point. It was the first time the government recognised its obligation to assist certain populations with healthcare. There were still concerns with the availability of healthcare with affordability, quality, and the accessibility of the healthcare system leading to scrutiny of the system's effectiveness. In the resulting decades, the confluence of technology, the rising costs of healthcare, and political controversy each factored substantially into the direction of the policies of healthcare for the country.

The attempt to address inequities in the distribution of care with the ACA in the last few decades along with new policies made for the accessibility and affordability of healthcare. Ideological fragmentation, however, remains a feature of the national conversation with discordant sentiments toward the government, the market, and personal accountability. It is critical for the United States to understand the growing volatility of the healthcare system. The historical factors and opposing viewpoints that contributed to the current healthcare system create a complex range of issues.

Philosophies of Healthcare: Right or Privilege?

In the United States, defining healthcare as a right or a privilege has been controversial and public. Those who claim healthcare is a right argue that every American citizen should be able to acquire necessary healthcare regardless of their socioeconomic status. Equally, every healthcare system should guarantee the right to healthcare access irrespective of a person's financial capabilities. This ideology sees healthcare as a fundamental human right that every nation ought to prioritise. In contrast, those who believe healthcare is a privilege advocate for the 'free thinking' side of the economy and the need for self-governance. They state that each citizen should strive to obtain healthcare. In addition, they argue that self-governed competition and consumer choices should be the dominant drivers for enhancement and effectiveness in the system. This ideology emphasises personal liberty and minimal state control over healthcare choices. They believe there should be freely competitive consumer markets which will encourage the people to be more cost-effective. The opposition of these two differing philosophies is the reason certain healthcare policies and practices in America exist. It is the basis for discussions on the Affordable Care Act, expanding Medicaid, and even proposals for universal healthcare financing systems.

In addition, it informs public perception concerning the importance of the government's role in guaranteeing access to healthcare for every citizen. As the policymakers try to bridge the ideological gaps, they are faced with the reality of inequity, the cost of care, and the obligations of the society in which we live. These and other diverse frameworks are instrumental to the active citizen who aims to contribute to the attainment of a healthcare system that is desirable and embracing to the members of American society.

The Healthcare Reforms Based on Market Principles from the Trump Administration

The market-based healthcare reforms from the Trump administration aim to reform the existing healthcare system with an aggressive focus on competition and market-orientated deregulation in a bid to lower the cost of care and widen access. Key initiatives included the rollback of the Affordable Care Act (ACA), association health plans and short-term, limited-duration insurance, and the advancement of health reimbursement arrangements. These policies were designed to enhance consumer choice, stimulate market competition, and lighten the regulatory burden on insurance and healthcare providers.

The foundation behind these reforms is the belief that providing people with the ability to make their own decisions regarding their health, while simultaneously creating a competitive market, will enhance outcomes and lower costs within the healthcare system. Supporters claim that these reforms support price transparency and market-driven healthcare, thus emphasising the individual and aligning with a free-market healthcare economy, improving system efficiency and responsiveness.

On the other hand, critics express fears regarding the potential negative impacts of the reforms on coverage, in particular on the most vulnerable persons and those with other conditions. The proposed abolition of the key provisions of the ACA, such as essential health benefits and the community rating regulations, has caused a stir with regards to the fairness and inclusiveness of the reformed system. Not to mention, the focus on the private sector as a solution, with the market-driven approach, has raised concerns about the level of consumer protection and the possibility of rising costs in the absence of comprehensive regulation.

It is important to study the policies in question and their effects on the population's health and the quality and affordability of health care and to draw real-world conclusions from them. It is one thing to seek efficiency and another to secure access to the minimum level of care that is and must remain essential for every citizen. This is a problem that, to be solved, requires an appreciation of the interaction between public and private sectors. As the discussion on the broader aspects of the proposed reforms is still ongoing, it becomes important to understand their effects on various segments of the population and the sustainability of the system as a whole.

Mamdani's Vision for Medicare for All

Mamdani's advocacy for Medicare for All takes on a whole new dimension because he firmly believes that healthcare is a right and not a service which can be rendered for profit. His vision is based on the idea that an ideal system of healthcare must be able to provide every individual, irrespective of their social or occupational status, with access to a full range of healthcare services without any barriers.

Mamdani's blueprint, formed from a wealth of data and conversations with health sector thinkers, attempts to remedy some of the most glaring inequities in the field of healthcare. Medicare for All attempts to reduce the administrative burden of private health insurance and out-of-pocket payments, thereby fundamentally reducing healthcare spending and guaranteeing that no one delays seeking needed care for fear of unaffordable bills, denial of coverage, or unpayable out-of-pocket costs.

Mamdani's blueprint focuses on preventive care and early intervention, which shifts the paradigm from reactive to proactive care in order to promote sustained health. In addition to the health of the population, this approach ensures that the entire system of healthcare in the country, and the costs of care, will be substantially reduced.

Also, his framework emphasises the need to negotiate reasonable prices for drugs and the need to control market consolidation to reduce the excessive commercialisation of the healthcaresystem. Unlike the corporate approach to health care, Medicare for All seeks to restore the balance of power in the system by reaffirming domination of patient care, care that is reasonable and useful and which is central to the system logic.

Recognising the connection between health and economic prosperity, Mamdani's foresight illustrates the extensive advantages of an effective public health system. Besides the health of a population, the proposed model seeks to reduce the burden of cost to employers and promote self-employment by removing the link between health insurance and employment, thereby enhancing flexibility and efficiency in the labour market.

In the illuminating notion of a Medicare for All system,

Mamdani is able to retain the notions of balance, unity, and advancement. In a sense, the notion ensures that every American has the basic privilege of necessary healthcare, which is a right, not a privilege reserved for the few able to afford it. As a society, we have a lack of compassion, and that is reflected by the lack of fundamental changes we have in achieving communal solidarity. We need to recognise that the health of every citizen is the responsibility of each and crosses the boundary of individual well-being to the well-being of the nation as a whole.

Comparative Analysis: Coverage vs Cost Control

During the debate on reforming healthcare in the United States, one dividing line is the extent of coverage offered versus the need to keep services manageable. Market-based advocates push the argument that the resource sink of healthcare is best stubbed out and left alone. On the contrary, Medicare for All proponents like Mamdani argue that the issue of access is a human right that needs to be defended and that any argument that is centred on access containment is bound to leave over half of the people without the most basic health services. In this case, his analysis for both approaches is troubling. Looking at countries with different healthcare systems provides insights into the dilemma of coverage and cost control in countries with universal healthcare. Some countries with universal healthcare have large parts of the population lacking support and funding for complex health systems. Other countries that focus on cost control often get criticised for the population that is uncovered or facing financial hardships due to extremely high out-of-pocket costs.

Furthermore, lags and inequity in healthcare access & outcomes outlined in these models reveal the subtleties of the relationship between coverage and cost control. Analysing the effects of these models on population health, it becomes obvious that no value-based cost control is not a guarantee for equitable access to healthcare, and conversely, no value-based broad coverage deals with the financial intricacies of sustaining such a system. Finding the right balance between coverage and cost control is not simple, and it is apparent understanding and managing the relationship of the intricacies of the healthcare system is crucial.

Such balance requires a structured strategy that preserves the cost containment elements without sacrificing universal accessibility and the quality of care. Moreover, broadening the analysis of the challenges to the social determinants of health and combining the results of behavioural and public health economics research will offer better structured frameworks for addressing these pressing issues. There is a need for the balance between coverage and cost control that will need to reflect the many facets of the population to ensure social, economic, and sustainability welfare, while pushing for the right balance between the health of the population and the finances of the healthcare system.

Impact on American Families: Important Case Studies and Testimonials

An examination of American households attempting to obtain and pay for medical care is a critical dimension of the analysis of the real-world consequences of healthcare policies. Understanding the fragmentation of the healthcare system in the United States would be aided by the analysis of robust case studies and rich testimonies. These narratives aid in comprehending the effects of healthcare access on both individuals and society at large. The Paterson family, living in rural areas sparsely populated by medical practitioners and institutions, is the focus of one of the case studies. While options are severely limited and out-of-pocket expenses are high, they face the dilemma of paying for and getting the care they need in the face of poverty. These narratives illustrate the geographical inequities and social system disparities that serve as a foundation for the healthcare system. In stark contrast, the public comprehensive healthcare testimonials emphasise the inequities that are accessible and available to people on the basis of socioeconomic issues. Such testimonies starkly emphasise how health inequities ease poverty for a large number of people. Through such case studies, it can be seen how robust healthcare policies that are present in developed countries aid those who are less economically developed.

These case studies highlight the importance of draughting policies that could alleviate the suffering of many families throughout the country. It also highlights the importance of access to healthcare in protecting the basic dignity and safety of people and families. There is a stark difference between the narratives and the reality that healthcare is not only about treatment and money but also about social justice and a basic human right. In these stories, it becomes very clear that American families need a healthcare system that does not increase their burdens.

The Role of Private Insurance: Is It Mandatory, or Is It a Roadblock?

The role of private insurance is something that has divided opinion, with some stakeholders arguing that it contributes positively to the development of the healthcare system while others think it does the opposite. Supporters of private insurance claim that it has brought choice, which is tailored to the diverse needs of the different clients; it enhances competition, which leads to technological advancement; and it improves economic efficiencies within the healthcare system. This is in addition to the fact that private insurance is necessary for the financing of hospitals and other healthcare facilities and the purchase of modern equipment and advanced technology, which, in turn, supports the delivery of healthcare services. The availability of modern and high-standard healthcare facilities and services is crucial for healthcare clients.

In opposition, some critics argue that the attempts by private insurance companies to provide every American healthcare as a right are flawed at their base level. They believe that private insurance companies contribute to the extreme administrative, billing, and other complex costs of insurance, as well as selectively avoiding ill clients, which leaves economically disadvantaged individuals grossly underinsured while wealthier people have multiple alternative insurance policies. Additionally, the avoidance of primary and public healthcare to increase profits is identified as a key factor contributing to fragmentation and irrationality in the healthcare system.

Private insurance supplements the healthcare system, making this concern particularly relevant. Proponents assert that this system benefits the economy by generating jobs and fostering growth. Furthermore, the well-documented nature of private insurance and its associated firms demonstrates how insurance companies use lifestyle incentives to promote self-directed care. In contrast, the other side argues that the profits of such companies come, in the first instance, at the expense of policyholders, resulting in a punitive cost, coupled with a family and individual level bare and, thereby, disposable income that is constricting, while the economy as a whole and, subsequently, consumer expenditure are, in the first instance, of concern.

The American healthcare system maintains private insurance in relation to patient choice, the functioning of the marketplace, and the equity of healthcare outcomes. Addressing this issue involves weighing the consequences of retaining and changing the private insurance system. The private insurance system in the United States remains an essential factor in determining the direction of healthcare access and affordability as ongoing discussions about reform continue.

In this case, healthcare access merits recognition as a measure of national progress.

Healthcare is a basic right. Like any other basic right, it should be given equally to all, no matter the situation. A country will only be deemed developed when its citizens enjoy basic healthcare facilities, which are the most accessible of all. A country that spends its effort and finances on tabulating and uniformly distributing basic healthcare coverage believes that its citizens and economy will remain thriving.

Furthermore, universal access to healthcare acts as a positive contributor to the economic development of a country. A healthcare system that offers preventive care as well as early diagnostic and treatment services acts to reduce the adverse effects that illnesses can have on a person's ability to be productive and the country's ability to generate economic value. With access to healthcare services and no financial burden, people can be active and productive members of the economic and social systems. Preventive healthcare also saves money for the individuals and the country that would have to be spent on expensive reactive treatment.

Universal healthcare is the result of the state's social contract with the people, showing the state's commitment to everyone's welfare. A country that is able to offer its people universal healthcare is also committed to ensuring that people are healthy, educated, and active participants in civic and economic life. Such a country is also able to strengthen social unity, eliminate health inequities, and improve the overall health of the country.

In addition, having unfettered access and universal healthcare is beneficial economically. In the international arena, most nations with universal healthcare have proven to have a higher degree of human development, innovation, and economic dynamism. This characteristic makes such countries more attractive for talent, investment, and collaboration, further enhancing their global standing.

Equally important, universal healthcare enhances a country's competitiveness and attractiveness in the global arena. The other benefits in scaling up investment and development also support the argument. This phenomenon is more pronounced in countries with higher human development.

To sum up, the value of access to healthcare is much more than a personal issue; the impact is national and also a true measure of the development, strength, and diplomatic ethics of a country. As outlined in this chapter, the value of a citizen's universal right to high-quality healthcare is a necessary condition of a country with advanced democracy and social justice.

Political Issues and Perception by the Public

In the context of the US, healthcare reform is more than a policy issue. It involves both political challenges and public perception issues. The political condition of the country significantly influences both the direction and outcome of each proposed healthcare reform. We currently live in a highly polarised environment, where there is deep partisanship. The powerful lobbies and the legislative bureaucracy make the enactment of any meaningful reform in the healthcare system extremely difficult.

The distinct and horizontal division of the functions of the private and public sectors in the arena of healthcare provision in the United States remains a significant source of tension and strife, constituting a political issue. The enduring ideological rift among reform advocates in the healthcare market is based on a minimalistic government approach that emphasises personal options and market freedoms. On the other hand, a singular approach in healthcare delivery, akin to the 'Medicare for All' model, as advanced by its supporters, makes a case for the broadening of the public sector for ensuring the right to healthcare for all citizens. Successfully navigating the deep conflict requires careful political skill and significant sensitivity to the various concerns and approaches of the multiple interrelated parties involved in the issue.

In addition to the other concerns that arise, the most prominent interest groups include those from the drug, insurance, and healthcare services sectors. Their financial capacity, integrated with lobbying influence, dominantly determines the shape of the entire healthcare approach at the level of policy and decision-making in the political arena. The dilemma of prioritising the public interest against the opposing interest that cuts across the population poses a significant and complex political challenge that demands a high level of attention and deep public interest commitment.

The public's perception of an issue positively influences the related concerns. From the perspective of the US populace, the healthcare system encompasses a vast array of beliefs, experiences, and expectations. This forum debates the testimony of any citizen, be they an academic or a member of the working class, as to the accessibility, affordability, and quality of the care given. For the public, crafting a health care bill is primarily an issue of communication. There is a need to construct a healthcaresystem that proposes policy options that the electorate is concerned with.

History and the experiences of other countries inform the public discourse, among other things. Colouring public attitude to reforms proposed is the history of this country and other contemporaneous attempts made in the world, as well as the attempts made here that were successes and failures. Furthermore, the public debate is influenced and made richer by the ability to think and discern other countries' systems of health care. These attempts to analyse the history of the subject and the experiences of other countries are something that the policymakers have to go through to earn the public's trust. These beliefs, as difficult as they are to discern, are important in garnering public enthusiasm.

To conclude, the crossing of political and public attitude avenues is surely the linchpin of instituting significant changes in healthcare systems. In the political and public spheres for which a policy is intended, it should seek to build a healthcare system that reflects the tenets of democracy, that is, fairness, kindness, and togetherness.

Looking Forward: Integrating Human Rights with Market Approaches

In predetermining the nationality of America's healthcare system, a guiding principle for policymakers, advocates, and the public is the combination of the market with the unique human rights. The relationship between the market and access to healthcare is a complex and delicate issue that needs to be addressed in years to come. In this section, we will explore the challenges and opportunities of the relationship between the two principles.

The fundamental question that remains is how to merge the economic principles driving a market-centered healthcare system with the moral obligations defined by the global human rights regime. This requires balancing the need to foster self-interest and competition as a means of promoting innovation and driving costs within market boundaries with the need to provide healthcare that is accessible, affordable, and of satisfactory quality to all. A new model can emerge by integrating market incentives with the responsibility to provide universal healthcare, which is a fundamental human right. Such a model would tap the entrepreneurial spirit of the market without fuelling exclusion and inequality.

At this stage, integrating current trends in technology and data analytics in the reorganisation of healthcare delivery and financing is critical. The willingness to invest in new approaches that improve resource allocation efficiency, increase system openness, and strengthen patient agency can increase empowerment at the same time as improving system sustainability. In addition, rethinking the legal and regulatory system to increase system accountability, consumer protection, and measurement of outcomes can help shift the market towards alignment with social value.

Achieving a balance between forces of a marketplace and human rights requires radical change and a rethinking of basic beliefs. The involvement of multiple stakeholders—public agencies, businesses, healthcare professionals, and the wider community—will be crucial to breaking down the siloed thinking that has so far prevented the building of a cohesive system that cuts across biases and ideological beliefs. Developing a system for joint thinking and evidence-based policy development and ongoing revision will be crucial to nurturing a healthcare environment that balances business with a social conscience.

In the end, the path forward requires thoughtful trials, purposeful boldness, and a deep dedication to the protection of the dignity and welfare of all people. The rethinking of where health is seen not simply as a product enables the construction of a healthcare system that integrates with the market, where the human rights of people are at the centre. The desire to create such human rights will motivate us to balance the forces of the marketplace with individuals' rights to self-fulfilment and self-ownership. However, as we eagerly explore changes that introduce market forces into this system, we face a significant challenge—and perhaps our greatest opportunity—of constructing a system that is both productive and just.

5
Immigration Nation
'Build the Wall' Meets Open Borders Advocacy

The Great Divide in American Immigration

The divide over immigration policy in America is not merely a political dispute but a profound rift in American society with regard to identity, belonging, and purpose. In fact, immigration policy is a proxy for deeper ideological rifts, and the divide over immigration policy is a proxy for the deeper rifts in the American psyche and the vision for the country. The immigration divide, fundamentally, asks the question: what country does America aspire to be? Unlike proponents of an open immigration policy, the advocates for stricter border controls prioritise national security, economic protectionism, and cultural preservation. In their eyes, the border immigration controls for America are the first line of defence for American values and interests. Contrarily, advocates of border liberalisation do not simply argue for an open border policy on immigration on the basis of inclusiveness. Instead, they argue fundamentally on moral grounds for the greater global interdependence that immigration creates. Immigration is a policy that can reinvigorate American society and economy and reaffirm America's leadership in the global human rights framework.

The divide I speak of here is not a question of policy alone; it is a question of who we are as a people, with consequences for the very fabric of the Republic, from schooling to work to health and beyond. The entire immigration system represents absolutely opposing attitudes a person can have toward patriotic sentiment, national identity, and America's influence abroad. The impasse over immigration acts as a benchmark for the complex issues confronting the American political system, including concerns about population shifts, the integration of the American economy into international markets, and a reevaluation of America's global influence.

Historical Context: America's Immigration Legacy

Immigration and the nation's legacy have always been interdependent, and America truly reflects the legacy in its core identity, from the times of European immigrants in the nineteenth and twentieth centuries to today. The arrival of immigrants in America, particularly through the forced migration of slaves, marks the beginning of America's true historical narrative. In the history of America, there are the Immigration Bronze Acts, the Chinese Exclusion Act of 1882, the Bracero Program, and the 1924 Act. These shifts in America's attitude towards immigrants and immigration itself are marked with fear and imprisonment, xenophobia, exploitation, and assault through guest worker programmes and labour. These all exemplify the systemic aggression and violence which are a result of the unresolved issues of the Native Americans, as they were the first ones to welcome the Irish, Italians, Jews, and Mexicans to America.

There has always been an internecine nexus of uproar over the migrants, and America has always been the main destination. America has always been confused over the question of why migrants choose America to escape to. In an effort to maintain the 'American' identity, America has always been the main target of assimilation and cultural appropriation. The public and current administrative system in place have always been concerned about the new arrivals to the nation, where restraint to the broad morals of America has become the main focus of debate.

The persistence of ethnic neighbourhoods with their bricolage of traditions, along with immigrant business activities, has anchored their impact on American life and culture.

One must also appreciate how American immigration policies have evolved in relation to other continents, influenced by various geopolitical and economic structures as well as moral responsibilities that have shaped reality.

The acquisition of territory and attendant international wars have created refugee solutions and enabled catastrophic movement of people across the earth. All such movement raises significant ethical dilemmas.

The history of American immigration policies stretches over centuries and reaches far and wide. The discussions that have dragged on for years on end about arbitrary and scientifically meaningless borders, caps on immigration, and amnesty seem trivial in the shadow of the grind of history. The waves of nativism in the US intermixed with nativism in the world have led to the disintegration of civilisation and culture. Nativism in the phases of self-defeat has created chaotic threads of civilisation worldwide. This history supports the thesis that nativism destroys civilisation. On the other hand, the resilience and contributions of immigrant settler communities still validate the American dream in relation to policies and politics. The criticism the world makes today about the policies of nativism in the US has deep roots. The history of American immigration comprises tensions and triumphs that underline the stories of refugees and self-seekers settled within the borders of America.

The Philosophies Behind the Wall: Security, Sovereignty, and Economics

The conversation about building a physical barrier on the United States and Mexican border concerns the philosophies of security, sovereignty, and economics. The supporters of the wall contend that it acts as a barrier for uninvited immigration, possible security issues, and the influx of unlawful goods, thus protecting the national interest. For these supporters, a fortified border represents national sovereignty, which includes the right to control immigration and defend a country's borders based on principles of self-determination and self-governance. Moreover, supporters of the wall highlight its economic implications, arguing that public jobs, wages, and resources demand border control for the sake of Americans and residents.

In contrast, people against the wall question these claims, stating that there are different methods to achieve border security, such as the use of technology, espionage, and diplomacy—none of which require erecting a wall. They claim that the humanitarian elements of immigration are lost and inadequate policies are set to the reality of the need to offer asylum to those escaping persecution and war. They also claim that any discussion of migration should not be limited to security and that there is a positive contribution to the economy and a cultural diversity that comes with immigration, and therefore, we need policies that are open to immigration and that appreciate international obligations.

Examining the philosophies behind the wall reveals not only a clash of policy preferences but also a deeper ideological divergence about the core values of and purpose of borders and nationhood. It epitomises a struggle between competing notions of security, identity, and economic interests, which situates the wall within a broader debate about the relationship between the state, its citizens, and the global community. Moreover, this controversy brings to light troubling dimensions of immigration policy, asking us to balance the fundamental right to seek safety and autonomy with the ethical obligations of humanitarianism, compassion, and justice. The proposed border wall serves a pedagogical purpose by inviting students of immigration policy to engage with the intricacies and contradictions of contemporary border policy as well as the competing perceptions of American identity and inclusiveness.

Open Borders Advocacy: Inclusion, Humanity, and Global Responsibility

Open Borders Advocacy offers a new perspective outside the scope of what is mainly regarded as immigration policy. It is grounded in inclusion, humanity, and global responsibility, and it challenges the restrictive nature of borders. It advocates a world in which crossing borders is a matter of a fundamental human right and is not merely a legal issue, rooted in the right of universal freedom and equal opportunity for all. The philosophy in this advocacy supports the notion that the worth and dignity of every human person is a right and should be enjoyed by all irrespective of birthplace and citizenship.

Supporters of open borders have based their arguments on

the ethical issue of the oneness of humanity. They argue that restrictive immigration regimes are the cause of inequities and injustices that deny people access to escape from poverty, violence, or environmental catastrophes. They argue that the inclusion of diverse people offers societal advancement in the appreciation of multiculturalism and improvement. They argue, too, that the advocates of open borders have to consider the history of the world, which is full of mass dislocation, forced migration and the consequences of colonialism as primary reasons that require a change in the way borders are conceived.

They consider strict restrictions on immigration to be acts of exclusionary nationalism that fail to recognise collective responsibility to tackle global issues.

Proponents of open borders understand the potential impacts of the economics of open borders and try to explain the myths associated with open borders' impact on the labour market, welfare, and public finances. They contend that borders stifle competition, mobility, and innovation, thereby impeding economic growth and underutilising the economic potential of immigrants. They also underscore the importance of implementing integration and public support policies for immigrants, as they strive to demonstrate that immigration bears a public cost. Open borders argue that the negative consequences of unlawful migration and the abusive capitalism of immigration should be eliminated, and in their place, humane and socially responsible immigration policies that emphasise immigration for the purpose of family reunion should be encouraged.

Within the borders of any one country, and in this case the country that advocates having no border restrictions, is the burden of the open border advocates, and they claim that the advocates of open borders owe a moral responsibility that is positive in the extension to every country, more specifically the rest of the world. They argue that wealthy countries have a positive obligation to correct and deal with the consequences, which are historical, and to be more responsive to the causes which create migration and conflicts leading to the migration of people. They promote the need for an international framework that can build the developed side of the world to guarantee that development will be equitable and ample opportunities available to everyone. In this way, they envision a world without borders where people have the freedom to travel and live without facing the consequences of oppressive immigration laws.

The idea behind borders being open is about having more access, being more humane, and having more interconnectedness, which makes much more sense, especially from the perspective of humanity and the responsibility we bear towards each other and the world.

Identity Politics and Nationalism: Constructing 'Us' Versus 'Them'

In relation to immigration policy, identity politics and nationalism, the 'us' and 'them' mentality is at the heart of much public conversation and government action. This assumption is particularly evident about who is in and who is out of the nation. The 'them' from a nationalist approach to immigration is who is 'othered' and in arch and often protective dominion over the 'native' in relation to race, ethnicity, and culture. The 'them' is often a figment of the imagination which serves to rally around the lie of a pure, national, and unified community under constant threat of dilution or replacement. And on the other side of the spectrum, identity politics, which is often an antithesis to nationalism, argues on behalf of the unrepresented and marginalised people of the community whose diversity is seen as a threat, providing an argument in support of their inclusion.

Equally salient, these elements within the context of immigration shape the development and execution of policies. The notion of border control and immigration intolerance, which is fiercely advocated, is a direct manifestation of nationalistic sentiments, aiming to strangle the boundaries of the 'nation-state' within and raise walls against 'others'. On the other hand, those in favour of a more liberal immigration policy base their arguments on the concept of 'identity politics' and the intertwining of humanity, holding a collective duty to shelter and share resources. This battle of ideologies creates a tangled and complicated web of immigration reform interests and values.

In addition, the construction of 'us' and 'them' synonyms, according to the context, pertains to the focus of political mobilisation and strategy of election. The protective 'Us' who feel threatened experience nationalistic sentiment as being protective, culturally, and economically. On the other hand, identity politics functions as a peripheral strategy for historically marginalised and excluded communities through representation, collective action, and mobilisation. Thus, the war of these two paradigms pertains not only to a political one but also to a social and moral one, as the implications extend beyond merely the boundaries of immigration policy. The paradox of identity politics and nationalism describes American society, its spirit, its construction, and the concern for the silence of its citizens who need to listen to the promise of equality and inclusiveness.

The Role of Race and Ethnicity in Immigration Policy

Differential treatment based on race and ethnicity has been instrumental in the formulation of immigration policies in the United States and has been a constant undercurrent in the construction of national identity and citizenship from the Chinese Exclusion Act of 1882 to the immigration debates of the 21st century. The incorporation and exclusion of various groups based on immigration and ethnicity strongly determine the immigration policies of the United States. The discriminatory remnants of history, such as the National Origins Act of 1924, which set limits on immigration on the basis of race and ethnicity, epitomise the extent to which immigration and settlement in the United States are matters of national interest. It also raises a number of issues concerning the historical treatment of indigenous peoples and the impact that slavery and the slave trade have had on America's demography. The concept of belonging and the question of who is able to define it are intricately tied to the remnants of slavery in the United States. The intersection of race, ethnicity, and immigration policy is crucial when examining immigration control and the more general issues of policy and admission.

Furthermore, the immigrant communities' experiences in the areas of assimilation, marginalisation, and socio-economic contribution have been subjected to the existing racial power structure and hierarchy, which have imposed boundaries and defined levels of acceptance among a society's members. Moreover, the policies of positive and restrictive migration control imposed by states have been considered the result of distorted and oversimplified views of race and ethnicity. Also, the intertwined traits of race and immigration in a country as an entity involve the constellations of obligations of the country regarding social justice and equity, as the administrative inequities and naturalisation could be the result of inequitable visa control policies and systems. It is important to teach the citizens of the country the historical and current importance of race and ethnicity in the country's immigration policies in the US to prepare them to apply rational and border policies regarding the complexity of migration issues and national identity immigration policies.

Narratives and rhetoric: Influencing Public Attitudes Towards Immigration

The language and narratives surrounding immigration, which have been subjects of debate, controversy, and media coverage among politicians, the media, and advocacy groups, significantly influence how the general public perceives immigration. Public perception and attitude towards immigration has, more often than not, determined the policies and actions that governments undertake. These actions and policies can range from embattled to downright accommodating, and the described perception of immigrants being 'threats' or 'contributors' has had a profound effect on the discourse on immigration. Such powerful words used to discuss contrasting narratives have been and still are used by media personalities and political leaders and have almost always had a tendency to shape public opinion and influence policy. Therefore, it is crucial to illuminate the stories and language employed and their influence on the development of immigration policies and public discourse. This phenomenon is best seen by the narratives that immigrants are a drain on social welfare, a threat to the security of the nation, and a vicious competition for jobs. On the other hand, these claims have significantly bolstered the demand for immigration and border control measures. Positive narratives have, however, been crafted to counter the narratives outlined above and adopt immigration policies that are more progressive.

Rhetorical strategies like dehumanising language, fear-mongering, and appeals to national identity primarily support the anti-immigrant position and defend restrictive immigration controls. In contrast, proponents of immigrant rights have used the narratives of compassion, human rights, and the ethical principle of providing refuge to the persecuted. Supporters of more liberal immigration policies use the personal stories and struggles of immigrants to illustrate the need to humanise the issue and counter negative stereotypes. These narratives shape public perception, but their influence extends to the treatment and integration of immigrant communities as well. The framing of immigration debates creates a narrative that either promotes mutual understanding and empathy or enhances the stigma and marginalisation of immigrants. These narratives also have fundamental consequences on the psychological and social integration of immigrant and host communities. The framing of these narratives and their associated power structures must be understood to dissect the substantial immigration discourse and achieve the empathy necessary to improve immigration policy. This section analyses the complex and intertwined relationships between narratives and public rhetoric that have shaped immigration discourse, and their consequences on individuals, communities, and society as a whole.

Impacts of Policies on People and Communities: Real-Life Changes

The implications of immigration policies are deep-rooted and touch the lives and communities of many across the country. Understanding immigration policies and their impact on the lives and the stories of the people involved remains necessary.

Policies on immigration have an impact on families. Controlling borders and deploying people from other countries can split families apart, causing deep emotional turmoil. Witnessing and experiencing the removal of immigrants from their parents, including family breadwinners, highlights the profound humanitarian issues associated with immigration policies.

Immigration policies also influence the behaviour of local residents and the various changes that occur in the community. The patterns of immigration to and emigration from a country, along with the policies implemented to control these patterns, have an impact on the ease of working in a particular country, along with the rest of the world. For example, the policies to restrict the migration of people with particular skills can have a direct impact on the industrial employment of those particular skills.

The economic implications of specific immigration policies are also a matter of concern. Prohibitive immigration policies may stifle certain branches of industry; thus, productivity is lost and economic expansion is stunted. On the other hand, liberal immigration policies may enhance the level of innovative and entrepreneurial economic activity. The linkage between immigration policies and economic results is complex and must be carefully analysed for policy formulation.

Furthermore, we express the effects of immigration legislation on integration policy and the internal unity of the country of immigration. Policies of integration and citizenship recognition enhance positive social cohesion and integration, while citizenship actively builds the identity of the country of immigration and, as a result, strengthens its social and national image. In contrast, integration policies focused on social exclusion may increase social fragmentation and disregard the basic principles of justice and equality, which the country is built on.

Last but not least, the evidence which supports the assumption that immigration policies influence policies of immigration and social integration, on the other hand, is that immigration and emigration, on the other hand, are policy. It unidirectionally shapes the conditions of life and the ambitions of people as well as the strategy and policies of the country. This helps us understand the real-life impact on the people of the policies being made and the stakes involved in setting the immigration policies.

Obstacles and avenues for mutual reform

The immigration system of the United States requires reform. Understanding the system's issues is one of the many challenges involved in immigration reform. One of the bipartisan challenges relating to this issue is appeasing the "Build the Wall" and "Open the Borders" campaigns. Since the beginning of time, people with entirely different views about border security, pathways to civility, and humanitarian issues have resulted in chronic stagnation in ideologies. These challenges do, however, provide the framework for those willing to create substantive reform for both sides.

The capability to construct immigration policies that best protect the country is still in an elusive phase. The immigration system has to provide for the people; it does not. The border enforcement policies, visa allotment, and asylum seeker policies are still open for debate and require cooperation in order for the country to reclaim its reign in compassion and protection for those on the other end of the axis of evil. The policies that govern undocumented people living in the country are another focal point which develops unambiguous, reasonable, and bipartisan responses which do not seem to exist today.

Supporting bipartisanship is the requirement to tackle the economic consequences of immigration reform. Both sides have recognised the immigrant workers' contribution to the US economy, alongside the legitimate concerns about job losses and wages decreasing. Moreover, bipartisan support on immigration policies that encourage skilled immigration and entrepreneurial investment will foster innovation and enhance America's competitiveness.

Responding to the alleviation of most of the legislative restraints about cross-party cooperation also means addressing the ethical issues of immigration. Some human rights advocacy organisations support the idea of reform that emphasises the restriction of the protective detention of people, family reunification, or members of the family being separated administratively who are unnecessarily vulnerable to detention. Achieving bipartisan resolve on predictable and uncontroversial issues like the resettlement of refugees and temporary protected status will require a bipartisan ethos towards international obligation and imagination to act to relieve human suffering at the international level.

Reform that attempts to meet these challenges holds great promise, as do reform opportunities that are not strictly partisan. Bipartisan immigration reform will come from constructive engagement, evidence-based policy research, and international policy learning and sharing best practices. There is also the promise of employing new technologies to improve border management, border surveillance, and border control operations to enhance national humanitarian values.

In addition, embracing public-end partnerships along with civil society can resolve the ideological gaps that progress has stalled on for decades. Bottom-up initiatives that aim for community integration, cultural diplomacy, and education are crucial in transforming public perceptions of immigration and forging connections among divergent political groups.

In the end, bipartisan obstacles and the pursuit of reform are best served by an approach that seeks to minimise the political noise and emphasise that collaborative effort is needed to work towards practical outcomes. Compromise, compassion, and a willingness to plan for the decades to come are vital for the immigration system to be coherent, sustainable, and, fundamentally, aligned with the guiding principles of the New American Century.

Conclusion: Addressing Ideological Gaps in the New American Century

As one attempts to disentangle immigration policy issues, one realises the breadth and depth of the ideological rifts in American society. The "walls" and "open borders" philosophies are but the tip of the iceberg of profound divergences about identity, community, and the very concept of Americanism. However, we must work collaboratively and constructively to narrow and bridge these gaps. The common vision of an economically prosperous country that welcomes its new immigrants and treats them as integral to society is one of the cornerstones that can make it an achievable goal, even if it means closing the gaps that have previously existed.

The closing of these gaps will demand honest work and investment from both sides of the divide. It will require understanding and providing answers to the fundamental questions of what the issues are, what needs to be worked upon, what the differences are, what needs to be unified, and what the approaches to immigration policy need to be. We need to balance the extremes of constructive disengagement and constructive engagement, offering asset-based approaches to inclusion that animate the discourse of the entire system.

To be effective, any effort to address America's immigration system must include policy approaches that encompass border control, economic consequences, and humanitarian concerns in both border and humanitarian policy. Each such policy must incorporate elements of cooperation and support for America's founding principles of equality, justice, and opportunity for all. There is a way to address these issues that does not involve extreme positions and does necessitate reasonable compromises. This approach is better for immigrants and America's citizens and leads to a more efficient immigration policy.

The unprecedented shifts in the demographic configuration of the United States in relation to the rest of the world and the high degree of globalisation entail, more than ever, a rethink of immigration policy as a form of national transformation. We must reshape our national identity to reflect what it truly is: an evolving mosaic of diverse people and experiences with many divergent facets. While celebrating such an identity, it is crucial also to address unfulfilled historical wrongs and offer not merely participation but active engagement and self-empowerment to build a community, a society which provides respect, dignity, and opportunity to all, which is the promise of America.

The gaps of separation, stemming from deeply rooted differences, may seem impossible to bridge. The opportunity for reconciliation and advancement for a new century that America offers is unparalleled. The neglect of rhetoric nurtures the radical empathy the country needs, embracing pragmatic solutions to cross the ideological divides of the gap. America's bold, redesigned, transformative vision is capable of achieving the sincere, equitable, and inclusive future that the citizens aspire for the country to represent. The future reaffirms the core values deeply etched in history while also meeting the values aspired to by those in coming generations.

6
Workers and Wealth
Tax Cuts and Deregulation Versus Wealth Taxes and Worker Cooperatives

Value creation and distribution in a historical context

Analysing historical context regarding value creation and distribution allows us to appreciate the development and refinement of economic theories and practices. During the mercantilist age, when the dominance of wealth and economy relied on possessing valuable resources, people viewed wealth from a zero-sum perspective. The mere possession of wealth was considered the epitome of success, which in turn shaped trade and acquisition policies. Their trade policies favoured acquisition, possession, and retention, thereby shaping the global dynamics of trade and power. Their power-stricken trade policies shaped the world we live in today. The shift to classical economic policies transformed the value base from land to labour. This brought a shift towards exchange and production, opening trade and value to an industrial capitalism attitude. The industrial revolution ushered in a class that is now employed in heavily paid jobs due to their possession of resources and labour. They've revolutionised the economy. Suddenly, the world experienced a global dissection that led to the advocacy of new policies aimed at ensuring proper distribution of the economy and trade. This era marked the beginning of labour-related economic policies. These policies shaped the global economy during the Second World War and the period following the Great Depression. With the end of the world war and the Great Depression, the world underwent rapid transformation. The policies were now rigid. Supply and demand favoured labour. The resources were now allocated to the labour force. The world was reshaped.

The birth of the Keynesian school of thought marked the first system of demand economics that focused on the essence of public spending and consumption-driven economic growth, whereas the neoliberal revival focused on supply-orientated policies and deregulation for fostering productivity and innovation. The last decade of the twentieth century's globalisation period changed the mechanics of value creation by adding transnational supply chains, reshaping the world's labour dynamics, and fostering discussions on living wages and ethical sourcing. These different periods in history have cumulatively advanced the issues of ease of access to wealth, distribution of resources, and the impact on society of different value creation methodologies.

The Influence of Tax Cuts on the Economy and the Theory of Trickle-Down Economics

Tax cuts are purported to stimulate investment and spur economic growth in the country while also alleviating the tax burden on the wealthy and corporations; this, along with increased investment and job creation, is expected to contribute to overall growth. The credibility of the theory 'trickle-down economics', which advocates tax cuts for the rich and corporations, has been a topic of heated conversations among scholars and policy framers in the economics field. Proponents argue that tax cuts lead to increased business expansion and, consequently, higher wages for employees. However, this assertion is challenged by several historical statistics that show a significant shortfall in the benefits available to the broader population. The assessment of tax cuts is complex and requires an in-depth analysis from both the macro and micro perspectives. It is argued that tax cuts at the micro level encourage firm investments in equipment, technology, and labour construction, which are on the rise. Additionally, these tax cuts are said to boost both firm productivity and the overall economy, leading to higher projections and increased investments that stimulate economic growth. At the micro level, lower individual rates of tax are argued to have a higher economic value, which encourages risk-taking, as it is also argued that the earnings of an entrepreneur who is willing to take risks must also be allocated to tax. It is also argued that individuals engage in entrepreneurial ventures. Moreover, investing such earnings in business will stimulate economic growth. The arguments supporting lower individual tax rates are weaker when evaluated from a proof perspective. There are assertions that the ultimate aim of tax cuts is to purchase shares and to pay executives rather than increasing the investments attributed to the employees.

Additionally, losing revenues from tax cuts could limit the government's ability to invest in vital public goods, like infrastructure, education, and social services, which could negatively impact growth in the future. The microeconomic consequences resulting from tax cuts also deepen the concern around the distribution of wealth. While high-income earners could enjoy significant benefits from having their taxes lowered, low- and middle-income earners would suffer from the inequitable distribution of gains in the tax system, which increases inequality even more. It is important to note that the consequences of tax policy are not simply financial; they fundamentally reshape structures and values in society.

The trickle-down effects of such policies must include an assessment of social mobility, cohesion and opportunity across generations. When evaluating the supporting perspectives and counterarguments, it is crucial to understand the actual consequences of tax cuts on economic growth and equity to effectively structure the debate.

Deregulation in Practice: Business Growth Approach

Deregulation, or the withdrawal of government control over the monitoring of an economy's activities, has been advocated for by followers of a laissez-faire approach for quite some time. Supporters of the view usually note that freeing an economy from regulation is positive, since it reduces bureaucracy, increases competition, stimulates new ideas, and therefore expands the economy and prosperity. What is undeniable, or in practice, however, is that deregulation has been a most complicated and multi-faceted phenomenon.

Proponents of the view claim that, by promoting free enterprise, deregulation works like a stimulus to business expansion. Within a deregulated economy, a company is not as free as it can be. It is still constrained by some rules, but it can make more autonomous decisions. In addition, deregulation in redress has been suggested as a technique for an increase in investment, since reduced bureaucracy and more efficiency in the red tape processes can attract capital from both domestic and foreign sources.

Critics, or those that look at it from the opposing view, point to the negative consequences of deregulation as the most severe. In the absence of regulation, profit is more important than sustainability, and an economy, along with its environment, people, and money, is prone to worse exploitation than is currently happening. In addition, increasing inequality suffers from a reduction in deregulated standards and protections.

The consequences of deregulation can be seen throughout history. The financial deregulation that accompanied the 2008 economic collapse is one of the more recent examples that highlight the danger of letting the market operate without barriers. On the other hand, many other examples demonstrate how the removal of regulation has inspired deregulated markets to innovate and intensely compete, thus advancing entire industries.

The current problem is that while customisation of regulation remains overdue, some aspects go beyond economic logic. There is a need to consider the impact of the proposed changes on society and morality. The main burden of balancing the need to protect the public interest and the need to stimulate economic activity falls on both policymakers and the public. The issue of how to go about deregulation raises the most fundamental issues of policy on the nature of regulation, the economic growth that is targeted, and the mechanism of distribution that is equitable.

Wealth Taxation: Principles and Potential in Reducing Inequality

Wealth taxation looks to solve the enduring problem of economic inequality and is quickly growing in popularity. The rationale for this lies in the progressive taxation systems where resources are shifted downwards from the population's apex to fund social welfare and inequality alleviation. The primary focus of wealth taxation conceptually is to change the resource ownership configuration through confiscatory taxes on the amassed fortunes of the ultra-rich. Quintessentially, economic stratification will be alleviated, and social cohesion and stability will be enhanced. In the opinion of proponents, excessive concentrations of wealth will disrupt social and economic systems, stalling social mobility and preserving privilege over several generations. With the intention to ensure equality in resource opportunity access, wealth taxes will diminish said wealth inequality. Besides the inequality reduction proponents, wealth taxation is said to be a fair system because the constituent's funding is proportional to the benefits accrued from it, and it's the responsibility of the beneficiaries to maintain the system. Wealth taxation, in this regard, is a fair taxation system that, in turn, serves to enhance the public purse to fund vital public expenditure, like education, health, and infrastructure.

It indeed lifts some of the burden from the middle and working classes and contributes to a more progressive and productive society. Unfortunately, some argue that a wealth tax may impede investment, new business formation, and economic growth overall. The concerns about capital flight and avoidance of income tax also oppose wealth taxes. Even more, the practical difficulties of ascribing and administering taxes on wealth pose unsolved implementation issues. These discussions illuminate the tension between the goals of policy, economics, and society. Understanding the relevance of wealth taxation to inequality requires serious analysis of cross-national data and other evidence. Wealth taxes in different countries play a role in closing inequality gaps and stimulating economic activity, revealing important lessons on their application. The discourse of taxation on wealth is increasingly arrested. This requires enhancing the understanding of the practical aspects of wealth tax so as to provide useful rationales for future policy and tax balance equity.

Worker Cooperatives: Democratising the Workplace for Value Redistribution

Cooperative companies are more than just internal institutions. They are economic units as well. Worker cooperatives are more resilient to economic downturns due to their long-term approach to running a business. Their social and ethical commitments to the community also help sustain the economy and foster social integration. These local virtuous economic cycles, in return, help bond the social structure and mitigate deep inequalities. Numerous studies across the world have shown that worker cooperatives contribute to economic resilience and social cohesion alongside equitable wealth distribution.

Case Studies: Global Approaches to Wealth Reform, Successes, and Failures

A look at the various approaches to wealth reform almost anywhere shows that the outcomes of such policies depend not only on the policies themselves but also on the socio-political framework that surrounds them. Case studies provide an opportunity to see the real-world effects of different approaches to unequal wealth distribution. Scandinavia is seen as an example of success because of its social welfare system. Such nations use taxation and public services to help promote more equitable nations. These nations managed to reduce national disparity and citizen wealth, but there are concerns about their lack of willingness to accept entrepreneurship and innovation. Country-states that have adopted deregulation and low government intervention are facing issues with wealth disparity and social mobility. There is also an effort on the part of some developing nations to alleviate inequities through such approaches as adopting profit-sharing schemes and inclusive economic growth. These newer approaches to social policies have shown that with some innovation, there is the possibility of making a positive difference to communities that are at the bottom of the socio-economic structure, combined with the possibility of fostering sustainable growth.

However, they also highlight the challenges of aligning reforms to deeply rooted economic systems. A more detailed examination of historical efforts to deal with wealth disparities reveals the many ways they were successful but also the many ways they missed the mark. The history of redistributive policies failing because of second-order effects, or backlash from dominant groups, is highly instructive for modern policy analysts. Also noteworthy are the policies of wealth redistribution that, on their own, have reduced economic disparities and increased the economic resilience of a country. These case studies provide a focused look at the processes of wealth redistribution and the effectiveness of the policies designed to achieve them. These cases illustrate the wealth redistributive system alongside all other systems of society, thus informing policy analysts on the need for carefully calibrated and flexible responses that are clear of the sophistication in policies and realities on the ground.

Labour Movements and Advocacy: Bottom-Up Policy Advocacy

Labour movements and advocacy undertake the preliminary work of advocacy to influence policies that govern the distribution of wealth and the rights appertaining to a worker. These movements have won, and continue to win, dominant policies of economic and social governance that provide improved terms of trade for workers in all lines of economic activities. By forming and mobilising workers to fight in unison, labour movements seek to make changes at the legislative and institutional levels to achieve social and economic justice.

The essence of labour movements centres on understanding the dignity of the workers and their rights. Systematic advocacy on behalf of labour unions and grassroots initiatives aims to remedy systemic inequities and the power disparities that exist within the labour market. Unlike traditional advocacy, these movements put the workers at the forefront of their struggles to address stagnated wages, precarious working situations, and the erosion of protections that workers once enjoyed.

In addition, inclusion in advocacy and policymaking to promote the protection of marginalised and under-represented workers, including, but not limited to, women, people of colour, immigrants, and those in low-income positions, is a hallmark of labour movements. These movements attend to the intersectionalities of advocacy for labour rights to discriminatory policies and practices and the lack of inclusiveness within the structures that span across sectors of the economy.

In combination with the immediate problems facing the workplace, engaging in continual advocacy for significant change to the economy is a hallmark of labour movements. This change includes the push to develop and promote new legislation that facilitates the growth and establishment of worker-owned cooperatives. These cooperatives provide alternatives to the traditional hierarchy of business structures. Support of cooperative enterprises promotes participatory and democratic governance in workplace relations, allowing workers to funnel their collective power towards ownership, decision-making, and profit-sharing.

In addition, most often, trade unions work directly with policymakers, community groups, and other organisations advocating for comprehensive labour reforms, which refer to the integration of advanced and adopted protective measures at all levels, with the detection and reporting of violations, the stringent observance of established standards of labour and mutual responsibilities, and the guarantee of humane and dignified labour for all. Through the maintenance of coalitions and alliances, trade unions and labour movements can exert their unified influence to accomplish trade union goals.

In summary, advocacy and trade union movements represent the strongest element of advocacy from the bottom up, which aims to keep the economy functioning in the interests of the workers and the economy. They actively support the changes in the labour and economic laws which are based on the principles of equity, mutual assistance, and respect for human beings, and which are typically used to defend democracy.

Public Perceptions: Workers and Wealth Myths and Narratives

Public perceptions related to work, wealth, and economic distribution tend to be shaped by powerful and enduring myths and by narratives of indeterminate proof. Such narratives define societal attitudes and perceptions, guide policy, and shape personal thoughts and attitudes about work, value, and rewards. Perhaps one of the most popular narratives is the conventional view of success, which suggests success is always and only the result of personal effort and hard work. Yet, success is often the result of hard work and effort. This narrative, however, tends to be blind to the existing systems of inequities and barriers that all workers face to equal opportunity access. This myth is stubborn and resistant even when confronted by evidence that clearly indicates that one is more likely to be disadvantaged socioeconomically because of inequitable structural and systemic barriers and inherited disadvantages. Formerly articulated, the systemic neglect of socioeconomically disadvantaged people is a monstrous and more virulent version of the beast, short-sighted and plodding, sociologically. Another equally dominant and popular myth is the hostility directed towards able-bodied workers on public assistance which, somehow, controversially, assumes that poverty and impoverishment are something that someone does. This is a wide oversimplification of the phenomenon because many people work and, in the process of working, are subjected to the abominable conditions of work, low wages, and systemic neglect in terms of just remuneration. There is also the almost universally held view that the disbursement of wealth is an economic resource of negative value to society, which is a net gain to society, somehow.

This myth often ignores the other side of the coin regarding the role of inherited wealth, speculative finance, and exploitative practices within particular industries, along with the undue lack of appreciation for the contributions of public sector workers, carers, teachers, and other professionals whose labour is often not compensated adequately. These myths shape public narratives and policy options and influence public attitudes towards taxation, welfare, and the dignity of work. In addition, they shape the popular image of worker cooperatives and wealth redistribution, seeing them as inimical to prosperity. These myths, in contrast, serve to deepen democracy and lessen inequality by expanding economic democracy. In interrogating and dismantling these narratives and myths, we can sharpen the analysis of workers and wealth and the economy as a whole. Correcting and changing public narratives is essential for ensuring that we are able to design fair policies in a society that values each individual's effort and pays them appropriately.

Comparative Analysis: Economic Effects of Opposed Theories

Within the heated discussion of wealth distribution and the

worth of a person's work, one very important detail that deserves consideration is the comparative analysis of the economic results of divergent theories. Analysing the data and case studies relating to the different treatments for workers and wealth provides pertinent information on the real-life impacts of certain policies and the philosophies behind them.

The policies of the tax cut and deregulation's proponents form one method of comparison, involving the economic results of regions that supported such policies. The analysis of the results includes several fundamental components, such as GDP, employment, income levels, and the well-being of the population. Conversely, wealth taxes and the promotion of cooperative enterprises present a stark contrast, providing insight into alternative ways of achieving economic prosperity and fairness.

As part of this comparison, it is necessary to analyse the resilience and sustainability of the economic systems. Conducting a long-term and short-term assessment of profit aids in analysing the approaches from both relevant and socio-economic frames. Additionally, the impact on the neglected sections of society and the rising income disparity serve as vital dimensions, illustrating the effects of contradictory economic systems.

Furthermore, using foreign examples can strengthen the comparative evaluation to demonstrate how different countries have dealt with balancing the interests of workers and wealth. Reviewing case studies from various cultures and geopolitical and economic systems helps collect the necessary insights and summarise the essential points. The advantages and disadvantages of wealth reforms across the globe offer a patchwork of experiences and, consequently, a refined perception of economic systems and their impact on society.

Examining how economic ideas shaped the actions of the labour movement, as well as how movements encompassed advocacy, aid, and labour, reveals the need to understand how such narratives around the economy influence the public and its policies. This does provide clarity on how economic ideas shape bottom-up mobilisation. This deepens the need to explore how the economic idea being analysed relates to the socio-political context.

Ultimately, it is through careful and reasoned comparison that we can demonstrate the economic consequences of varying outcomes of different theories. A strong understanding of the wide-ranging outcomes that ideological divides can have on the lives of people, as well as on assets, strengthens the debate that is needed and the decisions that should be made, both constructive and informed.

Looking to the Future: Imagining New Forms of Value that Impact Equitably

While envisioning an economic system that serves all of society, it is equally important to cultivate new forms of value that impact wealth distribution equitably. The opportunity to offer value rests on the confluence of technology, socio-technical systems, and ecological and sustainable development.

One possible path forward involves altering corporate structures by distributing the interests of stakeholders alongside profit maximisation for shareholders. If companies developed a governance model that genuinely cared for employees, the community, and the natural environment, they would help create sustainable value. This model change intends to merge profit motives with ethical and social obligations, thereby changing the narrative around profit accumulation for wealth to be advancement for all.

Moreover, the development of worker cooperatives, and the proliferation thereof, presents a growing opportunity for transformation of traditional employer-employee relations. Providing workers with cooperative ownership and governance structures enhances their economic power as well as helps internalise the spirit of economic democracy. This economic democracy creates a social order in which workplace relations are based on the appreciation of the value of the input rather than simply the wage as payment.

While imagining new pathways, it is necessary to deal with inequities through wealth taxes that aim to redistribute wealth to strengthen community-orientated wellbeing. History has shown that societal cohesion and curing dissatisfaction are achieved through strong taxes on wealth spent on education, healthcare, and public infrastructure. Furthermore, investing in protectable work and developed social security promises equitable growth dividends as well as a strong foundation for inclusive wealth creation.

This envisioned paradigm focuses on strengthening local economies through the development of community-rooted, sustainable enterprises. By incorporating social responsibility into business, we encourage the comeback of keen economic activity coupled with responsible resource use along with the emergence of new ethical growth corridors. These local economic systems promote eased innovation, robust interdependence, and community self-determination, along with the creation of growth and prosperity networks.

Based on these possible future paths, it is the unwavering intention to take technological progress to support inclusive growth that remains most important. The use of digital technology for the equitable provision of market access, skill training, and financial services has the potential to elevate the most disadvantaged members of society. This embrace of technological inclusion gives people the ability to access and benefit from value creation, thus lowering the barriers to entry and increasing the overall effectiveness of participation in the economy.

In weaving together value creation and future trajectories, it is important to acknowledge that the development of value creation is to some extent the responsibility of society. The adoption of restorative resource use and consumption recognises the interdependence of the economy and the environment. This, together with the adoption of appropriate mechanisms for wealth creation, ensures that the ecocentric values of society are sustained. Such values will guarantee society value creation that is in harmony with the environment.

Equitable models of value creation can chart new trajectories shaped by value creation mechanisms for future innovation. Such mechanisms would integrate value creation and value distribution in a way that harmonises economic value and broad-based societal prosperity. We would then have the potential for a new, dynamic, and inclusive model of wealth creation that unlocks new economic frontiers of innovative economic, environmental, and social prosperity for all.

7
Climate and Future
Energy dominance versus Green New Deal

Mapping the Differences in Climatic Contexts: Past Narratives Versus Present Contexts

While the climate debate had its origin in the 20th century, it only gained prominence in contemporary discussions in the 21st century. The span of centuries in between was crucial, with the IPCC in 1988 acting as an epicentre, as it focused on the repercussions of climate change with the aid of scientists and politicians. The result was a series of treaties like the Kyoto Protocol and the Paris Agreement that aimed to curb the rise in temperatures and slow the increase of greenhouse gases within the atmosphere. Ever since, the debate around climate change has been full of political controversy, as people with different political leanings try to make sense of the debate in their own way. There are conservatives as well as liberals, and their positions on the matter are distant from each other. The overwhelming presence of climate change has become an issue of contention, especially in debates or discussions regarding the types or series of treatments proposed to tackle the issue. The intersection that lives between the science of climate change and political party constructs has become profoundly complex, thus shaping the lenses through which the public views these issues and the policies that are brought forth. The discussion about the impact climate change has had on history has shown the complexity of the challenge and the multitude of various people and organisations that came to dispute the history and the direction the narrative wants to take.

Energy Dominance Explained: Policy Branch Plans of the Trump Administration

The hallmark triad of the energy dominance approach during the Trump administration consists of fossil fuel-focused strategic expansion, elimination of restrictions, and quickened domestic energy production. With this, the short-order elimination of the Clean Power Plan and the repeal of restrictions on the flaring of methane, along with the diminishment of other environmental "obstacles" to energy development of these paranoid ecologists, have been the focus of key policy pivots. Furthermore, the relentless drive to increase the production of oil and gas has been illustrated by the efforts to unleash drilling and other extractive processes on the federally owned land and jurisdictional waters. This augmentation strategy intends to increase the energy independence of the country while at the same time maintaining American hegemony over global energy markets. It is within this context that the advocacy in support of coal, oil, and gas industries has been positioned within the broader framework as being essential to economic development and job creation, especially in the energy-poor areas of the country. This is done through the lax regulatory approach to the use of free enterprise systems, fully expecting that the investment of the sector and the resulting energy infrastructure will warrant the prosperity these policies richly deserve. Enhanced the geopolitical and trade policy as instruments of the narrative of the dominance will oil the gears of American energy exports while trying to influence the world energy market.

Critics, on the other hand, claim that it reveals a tendency toward short-term profit at the expense of sustainability, worsens climate change, and ignores the promise of renewable energy. Much of the discourse has been about the consequences of focusing on fossil fuels on the environment, population health, and the shift toward cleaner and more robust energy systems. The differing views on energy dominance mirror deeper divides in social and political issues, requiring deeper consideration of their consequences for the economy, the environment, and generations to come.

The Green New Deal: Visionary Ambitions and Policy Proposals by Mamdani

Recognised by many as a visionary framework, the Green New Deal, as outlined by Mamdani, seeks to strategically resolve the intertwined problems of climate change and economic disparity. For the sake of economic justice and environmentalism, this groundbreaking proposal aims to overhaul the entire energy infrastructure of the United States and integrate new bold policy approaches. The Green New Deal's objectives entail investing in the sustainable infrastructure of the country to foster the creation of millions of jobs, all in a legal and economically sustainable framework, to ensure the United States of America transitions into a carbon-neutral economy. This deal, with special emphasis on environmental justice, seeks to counter the inequities of systemic oppression through visionary inflection. The Green New Deal seeks to conquer the deep and embarrassingly embedded inequalities of climate change for climate-vulnerable peoples and maintain intergenerational, eco-social justice throughout the climate framework. This proposal, in the way addressed by Mamdani, exemplifies the moral obligations tied to climate change: acting upon the needed climate change.

At the heart of the Green New Deal are plans to restructure the nation's energy infrastructure, invest in renewable energy resources, and increase energy efficiency in multiple sectors. Using public expenditure and innovation, Mamdani imagines an America that has restructured its energy architecture, improved its climate, reduced carbon emissions, and reduced climate change overall. The Green New Deal also suggests that the nation has the right to clean air and water, which should also be freely available as a matter of social justice.

The Green New Deal covers more than just the environment, as the policy proposals contained in it represent a more thorough re-engineering of the economy of the United States. The Green New Deal expects that, with the right investment in clean technology, infrastructure, and human capital, economic growth can be achieved, which would also strengthen the nation's competitiveness as well as the resilience of its communities. Mamdani's vision of the Green New Deal illustrates the strength of the U.S. – and its people around the world – in the fight to eliminate inequality with the use of clean energy sources and narrowing down the gap with inclusive development plans.

Navigating climate policy entails crafting a proper action plan that aligns with the scientific evidence on policy proposals. While the Green New Deal engages with the work of environmental scientists and other specialists, it aims to go beyond the political wrangling and entrenched interests that lead to policy stagnation. The backbone of this approach is an adherence to evidence and scientific approaches, reflecting Mamdani's focus on rational, actionable plans that capture the optimal approaches and leadership in the discipline.

In essence, the Green New Deal integrates what is perhaps the most innovative of Mamdani's proposals on ensuring environmental sustainability, economic advancement, and social justice within an equally inclusive and prosperous country as the foundation of a new, optimistic, and inclusive vision for America. The Green New Deal, with its wide-ranging policy proposals and ambitious goals, reaffirms the core climate action principles of Mamdani as it aims to redefine America's climate policy, representing the equally critical anchor to Mahdani's vision for an America that is just and sustainable.

Scientific Consensus and Political Rhetoric: Analysing Evidence and Argumentation

In the current heated political scene, the debate over the existence of climate change becomes, more often than not, a conflict over proof and rhetoric. It is important to point out that the overwhelming majority of climate scientists believe that anthropogenic climate change is real, as evidenced in many documents such as the Intergovernmental Panel on Climate Change (IPCC) assessments. The problem is how to communicate this scientific consensus in a world filled with competing narratives and misinformation tactics. The over-politicised nature of climate science, and the societal perception of it, affects the 'truth' about it. Political figures greatly influence the attitude of the people towards climate change polar denial by denying the existence of science or mitigating the science of it. Grasping such complexities is crucial to untangling real policy questions from political posturing. By addressing the problems, we can improve public conversations to be less divisive and more evidence-based. It also requires a constructive shift in the debate on the paramount role of policy and the degree of public confidence in the science.

While analysing the intersection and gaps of the scientific conclusion and the political arguments, it is clear that any further meaningful progress in the battle against the climate crisis is hinged upon breaking the silos of partisanship and fostering a willing partnership in the advocacy of facts. In addition, the other part of the advocacy that is equally important is the need to explain to stakeholders the risks that come with ignoring the facts and succumbing to political rhetoric and the need to equip stakeholders with the ability to differentiate between truth and fallacy. It is very important to note that the inexpedient political gain is neither of wide value nor should it overshadow the facts because climate change is a problem that touches on every part of society irrespective of political polarisation. It is, therefore, a problem that every part and every stakeholder should take part in genuine responsible conversation. In the end, the polarisation of facts and political rhetoric around climate change is a clear call to action to move any climate policy that is sensible, irrespective of the source, partisan or not, from the mud of politically motivated arguments and frivolous antagonism.

Economic Impacts: Examining Employment, Economic Stability, and Growth Opportunities

Decisions made on environmental policy actions, especially on energy and climate matters, have important effects on the economies of the world and individual countries. In this paper, I will explore the effects of environmental policies on the economy, particularly focusing on employment, market stability, and growth potential. First and foremost, the demand for renewable energy and sustainable technologies will result in the creation of new jobs and employment opportunities in many industries. The development of new clean energy infrastructure investments in wind and solar power will help the economy to create thousands of new jobs in the range of construction, manufacturing, installation, and research and development. In addition, the growth of green industries will require people with new skills; thus, countries will have to improve their educational and training programmes to cater to the needs of the new green workforce. At the same time, the relationship between policy actions that are considered to be protective of the environment and market stability is also very thoroughly studied. The more diversified the sources of energy, the more the net is reduced on the range of carbon emissions, which will help to shield the economy to a considerable degree from the negative consequences that come from the over-dependence on fossil fuels and associated geopolitical developments and tensions.

Alongside these factors, guidelines focused on advancing sustainability and climate resilience provide strategic, long-term assurance for firms and financiers, which reduces market volatility while directing capital flow into progressive, sustainable investment opportunities. Finally, fostering innovation and advancing technologies through the adoption of sustainable practices can stimulate considerable economic expansion. More investment and commercial activity can be generated by adopting cleaner and more sustainable forms of energy and enhancing business practices. Also, the integration of sustainable practices into business frameworks creates opportunities for economic diversification, which enhances the global competitiveness of nations. Therefore, while grappling with the restoration of ecological integrity and economic progression, it is important to analyse the cross-connections of these domains. By recognising the interdependence of economic growth with the social policies fostering environmental protection, it is possible for governments and societies to devise means which properly socialise environmental conservation with growth and the subsequent distributive justice.

Intergenerational Equity: Balancing Present Needs with Future Responsibilities

An individual must practice intergenerational equity when making environmental decisions, balancing the needs of the present with the preservation of future generations. This is guided by the principles of equity. Mamdani's policies, which advocate for sustainable practices, effectively embody the principles at stake for the world that are compromised by inadequate sustainable policies. In this case, Trump's policies, which focus on short-term increases in economic growth and dominance in the energy industry, tend to lose sight of the impact they have on future generations and the environment.

Intergenerational equity goes beyond the mere preservation of the world's resources. It entails social justice and the complexities of equity and the distribution of gains and losses over time. Mamdani, borrowing from the democratic socialist school of thought, espouses an environmental policy that seeks to redress the climate justice deficit by empowering the most vulnerable communities. In the case of Trump, the administration's policies have particularly been criticised for deepening the environmental justice gap and ignoring efforts to dismantle structural inequalities around the world.

It is important to recall that when looking to the future, the decision-making of the present must integrate innovative approaches, that is, the essence of intergenerational equity. In this context, Mamdani's alignment with the need for far-reaching reforms, including the Green New Deal, highlights the importance of novel ideas as well as the need to fund and develop cutting-edge technologies that actively reduce the environmental impact of the economy. These initiatives position the current generation as the primary beneficiaries of policies that ensure environmental sustainability while concurrently demonstrating the prospective social responsibility of providing future generations with a world that is still habitable.

Lastly, while discussing intergenerational equity, the focus must shift towards understanding the intricate multi-layered ties that bind together the ecological, social, and economic subsystems. This is what Mamdani means when he argues for policies that consider the justice dimensions of the environment, because, as he notes, climate change is not just a matter of addressing environmental issues. In stark contrast, the simplistic exploitation of the environment manifested during the Trump presidency has been widely criticized—not just for the environmental consequences but for the lack of consideration for future generations and marginalised populations.

The consideration of equity between generations is a prominent concern when dealing with divergent approaches to any particular aspect of environmental policy. Equity between generations takes on particular significance, as it enables one to focus on social obligations to policy issues that concern elements of the immediate future as well as those that reach further down the temporal axis. The boundaries of intergenerational equity serve as a balance between current obligations and the perennial responsibilities of the policy in question and they ascertain in which directions the available policies deviate from proper environmental governance.

Technological Innovations: The Role of Advancements Toward the Attainment of Ecological Objectives

Amidst the climate crisis, the use of technological methods has surfaced as an important determinant of sustainable environmental practices. In this regard, understanding the role of advancements in technology is crucial in assessing its potential to reduce environmental degradation and promote a sustainable future. The progress of technology has enormous potential to alter the future of the planet positively through the adoption of various renewable energy sources, including solar and wind power, as well as breakthroughs in energy storage and efficiency. The adoption of smart grids, energy-efficient and low-emission transport systems, and advancements in carbon capture and storage also demonstrate the potential that technology has in addressing climate change. The fusion of information and communication technology (ICT) with environmental conservation has also enabled the use of technology for real-time and predictive resource management and ecological footprint modelling through big data. The use of advanced artificial intelligence, machine learning, and the Internet of Things (IoT) offers extraordinary prospects for the improvement of environmental monitoring, risk assessment, and management frameworks. The reduction of emissions and waste and the conservation of natural resources are also achieved through the implementation of sustainable strategies in agriculture, urban development, and manufacturing practices.

The adoption of new pristine technologies like advanced recycling and green materials changes the design of industrial operations and develops circular economies focused on the efficient and sustainable use of resources. Moreover, work on eco-friendly alternatives and breakthroughs in green chemistry and bio-based technologies explores new opportunities for patterns of sustainable production and consumption. A fully integrated, interdisciplinary approach to pioneering technology—blends of engineering, environmental science, and policy—can easily and profoundly impose the shift to a low-carbon, climate-resilient future. Technology can resolve current challenges, but there are social, equity, and environmental consequences to consider that must be rectified to ensure protection and fairness for future generations. International cooperation, knowledge sharing, and capacity building are critical in cross-border problem solving to upscale pioneering approaches and align collective actions in the pursuit of common environmental objectives.

International Perspectives: Impact of the US on Global Climate Policies

The impact of America's policies and practices on the environment is profound. The United States is an economic and political juggernaut and leads the world in framing climate policies. America's climate policies and their interplay with global legislative frameworks are complex and warrant in-depth examination. This subject matter seamlessly intertwines with our primary focus areas.

America's greenhouse gas emissions footprint, coupled with the United States' role in the Paris Agreement, is none other than the keystone of the nation's impact on the climate policies of other countries. This Paris Agreement, including subsequent diplomatic undertakings, alongside the responsibilities of the nation's climate furnished in the primary policy, is of utmost importance in formulating America's global climate strategy. This further leads to pondering America's foreign climate policy. The US foreign policy is split on cooperation with allied countries and siloed autonomously. The same applies to how US foreign policy structures its climate initiatives based on leadership parameters.

Additionally, understanding American perception and priorities about climate change discourse involves understanding the intricacies of selected diplomacy and negotiations. The intricacies of climate diplomacy highlight how domestic and international climate agendas intertwine, ranging from partnerships with emerging economies to dealings with old allies. In addition, the regulation of cross-border emissions, the transfer of technology, and the financing of climate mitigation and adaptation all acknowledge America's centrality in promoting fair and equitable global climate action.

In addition to formal diplomatic relations, the functions of American non-state actors, including corporations, research bodies, and advocacy groups, require more comprehensive analysis within the frameworks of climate change governance. Their actions within the technology circulation, investment, and knowledge systems contribute to the formulation of international climate change policies, illustrating the complex economic, scientific, and political underpinnings of climate action.

In conclusion, America's impact on global climate policy is not just about the direct consequences of U.S. actions on the climate. It is also about the opportunities for cooperation and joint responsibility in confronting what is perhaps the most challenging aspect of human existence. This analysis will enable more people to grasp the complexities of national and international climate actions and how they relate to contemporary climate governance.

Opinion and Activism: Climate Change Policy from the Bottom Up and the Middle Out

Public opinion and activism are critical in advancing policy relating to climate change. Driven by concerned citizens, grassroots movements seek to promote the optimal protection of the environment and prudent management of natural resources. Therefore, these movements stand a chance of shaping the policy positions of the government and commanding the political agenda. Through the building of public interest and support, grassroots movements stand a better chance of influencing the agenda of the government and political system, suggesting more positive steps in climate change action.

Following the expansion of youth movements and environmental advocacy groups, there has been an increase in the demand for bold and immediate reactions to climate issues. These and other movements, which are well known for their creative approaches to social media and grassroots organising, have rallied for major policy and corporate practice shifts. They have also elevated public discourse on the need for comprehensive approaches to combating climate change and the transition to more sustainable energy.

Public opinion also functions as a gauge for the success of implemented climate change policies. In general, the analysis of climate policies and public reports reveals the public's perception of climate issues, which climate policymakers use to assess the major concerns and priorities of the population they serve. To create a responsive climate change policy, public opinion should be strategically harnessed to ensure the needs of the various constituents and cross-sections of communities are met.

The responsibility of climate activism also infuses the people with a sense of ownership, which encourages them to think and act democratically. Activists come together to accomplish common goals, which in turn helps them use their collective power to demand institutions and businesses take responsibility for their ecological damages and promote accountability and responsible business conduct. In addition, they promote a culture of public environmental accountability and responsible citizenship. They collaborate to ensure that both the public and the government actively engage in environmental sustainability through appropriate and integrated policies.

To conclude, grassroots activism and public opinion are integral for making climate policies more vertically sustainable and accountable. The way people come together to mobilise the governance of the environment and the conduct of business demonstrates their collective power and the importance of such collectives in supporting and creating a tangible impact. Understanding public opinion as well as activism advocating climate policies is vital to build a responsive framework to climate change and enable constructive interaction with society.

Future Directions: The Possibilities for Bridging Starkly Opposing Climate Narratives

In the case of the conflicts surrounding climate change and the sustaining of policies related to environmental issues, what are some of the possible future paths we could take with regard to climate policies? In the case of climate change, the narratives of energy dominance and the Green New Deal are at the extreme ends of the spectrum and, as such, are very challenging but also embrace the great potential for novel solutions. One of the possible solutions to this problem is to promote and engage in what could be considered 'friendly and radical detractors' debates, or in other words, constructive debate in which the sides do not argue, but, precisely the opposite, try to build a coalition in order to produce some solutions to the problems that concern all of them. In other words, we are talking about establishing forums and other types of platforms for constructive debates, where, in particular, all sides to the questions try to persuade and have contested discussions.

Additionally, embracing and seeking a fusion of various disciplines will be important in the quest for what is reasonable and what types of comprehensive functions can be extracted. Davis is a synthesis of science and ethics and includes social, economic, and advocacy dimensions, which is why this synthesis can be used as a pivot to anchor policies and decision-making that at least attempt to formulate – and do not ignore – the broad, systemic climate issues of the matters that a large number of other points of view. Perhaps such a comprehensive and integrated mindset is what is needed for climate policies so that decision-making can be constructive and engage with those who will attempt to create solutions that are rational and reflective of the many contextual and constituent factors.

Furthermore, being open to new ideas and new technologies on how to cope with the shifts in climate sciences provides great opportunities for climate narrative integration.

Focusing on the use of clean mixed energy, the advanced use of carbon capture and storage, and the research and development in green technology can become rallying points above the divisions. A broader agreement on the role of technology in climate change and its impact can facilitate the processes of consensus on very different approaches.

Alongside this, global climate governance continues to be complex and demands cross-border collaboration, as well as diplomacy. Negotiated partnerships, combined with the complex multilateral launch of options, the free circulation of ideas and the blending of national and transnational debates, can facilitate the climate narrative integration on the world stage. Different facets of diplomacy can allow for the integration of starkly different policies, aiming to address the cross-border climate issues and demonstrating the possibility of agreement and collaboration.

The pathways that climate policies will take will ultimately depend on the innovative, practical, and inclusive solutions that are proposed, perhaps countering the contradictory stories that the climate change narrative has to offer. Implementing technological advancements, embracing diversity of thought, and promoting interdisciplinary collaboration and international cooperation will all be crucial to developing a 'one world' policy on climate. These future directions will be essential to formulating integrated climate policies that are sustainable, equitable, and enduring.

8
The Media Wars
How Each Uses and Views Media

Platforms and power

Media has played a central role in the construction of political power from the beginning of time; the spread of information and stories has helped shape people's attitudes and granted power to those in charge. From the first prints of history to the first television broadcasts and beyond, the old-school methods of media communication influenced the outcomes of politics and society as a whole. From the mid-90s onwards, the internet and the invention of digital technology have revolutionised global communications and triggered changes that all politics have to adapt to.

Any analysis of the digitisation of political communication must start from the standpoint of democratisation and decentralisation of the public domain. The first democratisation of communications technology and social media has enabled the Internet to remain a self-cleaning platform and provided limitless access to differing arguments, perspectives, and opposing opinions. Traditional media institutions with their 'gatekeeping', now collapsing, powered alternative stories, counter-narratives, and citizen's networks all to gain and lose traction at the same time on the world stage. Most importantly, the digital public sphere's unique centrality empowers people on a global scale with the timely access to make instantaneous changes and amendments to actions that they support.

The speed at which technology evolves has made it easier to spread authentic and misleading information that sways and influences people, even during elections. 'Fake news' and algorithm-controlled content illustrate how misinformation can spread and raise questions about democracy. Furthermore, the integration of news and entertainment has made it increasingly easy and popular to mix the two, further complicating the role of the media in political communication.

During these changes, the growing disparity in media exposure and literacy has exacerbated inequalities in political representation and engagement. How people and institutions can use the internet and social media to spread their ideas has changed the dominance structure in the politics of a country, raising questions about the representation and equity of democracy.

It is important to understand how media and power are used together in their relationship to one another. This is to encourage the study of how political communication has changed in the past few decades. An analysis of the media's influence on democracy and political society must account for the historical and current realities of the media and democracy's relationships, as the impacts are bound to be societal integration.

How Political Communication Has Changed with Technology

Technology has changed almost all aspects of how humans communicate with one another. Political communication is no exception. Social media networks and other digital platforms have brought about a global shift in the transmission, understanding, and engagement of information. In addition, the evolution of digital media has paved the way for people to actively engage with political leaders. This, in turn, transformed the structure of political communication. Unlike social media platforms, people's access to engagement with newspapers, TV, and radio was confined to a passive observership. Politics was deeply controlled, with public opinion being a powerful currency. Moreover, the orthodox methods of communication bridged the gaps and empowered leaders to directly communicate with their supporters. Passively, leaders defended their traditional methods of communication. Politicians directly engaged with the public. In this digital phase, the politicians communicate directly with the public. Communication is more rapid and crucial and has infinite dimensions of visibility. Furthermore, the use of algorithms in social media has transformed the way people approach political posts and arguments. Politicians are able to access a higher level of surveillance in controlling their followers and opponents.

The ease of spreading information online has made the reach of both truths and falsehoods wider than ever before and made the task of distinguishing between them increasingly difficult. Social media has transformed the style of public discourse as well as the processes of public agreement and mobilisation by becoming the main spaces for the articulation, debate, and advocacy of social and political causes. At the same time, however, the same social media has become a source of anxiety because of the problems of echo chambers, filter bubbles, and the disintegration of a common social reality. In addition, there is a continuing concern about the political processes and outcomes in the context of the ever-changing world of the new technologies of communication and the corresponding political dynamics. Such changes in communication and public participation patterns call for the intersectional and interdisciplinary analysis of technologies, media, and politics in light of the new rational, ethical, and reflexive frameworks that help in the preservation and enhancement of public debate and social discourse.

Trump's Twitter Strategy: Direct Engagement and Controversy

Trump's use of Twitter is revolutionary and has changed how communication and politics intertwine in our time. He tweets on a daily basis and has over eighty-eight million followers who receive his posts. He also includes policy outlines, public opinion, and attacks on his rivals in his tweets. By strategically using Twitter, he communicates with his base and goes far beyond it, thus avoiding traditional means of communication. In addition, he has succeeded in attracting attention but has also invited unnecessary criticism. By starting personal attacks with no evidence, he has raised concerns about the best way for a president to communicate.

Because Twitter is real-time, he has been able to transcend boundaries, and his tweets dominate the public sphere and the news. On a viral basis, he posts threatening tweets to leaders of other countries and also mocks his political challengers and rivals. He tweets in a way that always seeks to provoke them, and at the same time, his posts fulfil other agendas. These strategies are easily recognised and allow him to elevate governance to a viral level, resulting in impulsive behaviour.

Additionally, the combative and divisive nature of most tweets has both aimed to deepen division and succeeded in doing so, often involving accusations of false claims and fostering animosity. The lack of nuance in the 280-character tweets has sparked concerns about the erosion of democratic principles and the decline of civilised debate. Trump's unrivalled, unconventional, and controversial use of Twitter has perpetuated disputes, stifled rational policy debate, and sustained the narrative of unresolved wars.

In this regard, the so-called social media diplomacy practiced by Trump has, despite criticisms, devalued the entire public discussion and instead cultivated an unrestrained atmosphere abundant with falsehoods and lies. Furthermore, the continuous targeting of the media and journalists has cast a shadow of suspicion on established media outlets, undermined their credibility, and reinforced a self-sustaining cycle of misinformation.

Trump's use of Twitter as the primordial means of communication by a president has most certainly changed the aspect of how politicians interact with citizens, having mitigated severe negative responses. The softening of the consequences through the use of electronic media and ceaseless defences of the ever-growing turbulence of the political atmosphere have certainly changed the perception of political communication on the net.

Mamdani's Grassroots Approach: Mobilising through Shared Narratives

Mamdani, as a case study, embodies a grassroots mobilisation strategy for engaging with media on the basis of a shared narrative. While Trump tweets in a more direct and often confrontational manner, Mamdani focuses on community building and relationship development through narrative and dialogue. His emphasis on the importance of engaging with a wide range of perspectives for social change captures the spirit of social justice advocacy. Mamdani uses media, not as a tool for broadcasting messages, but as a platform for mutual learning and co-creative empowerment.

Mamdani's media strategy focuses on the deliberate construction of narratives that align with the realities of the lives of the most marginalised. In the public conversation, Mamdani seeks to shift the frame and focus on narratives that are neglected or misrepresented in dominant discourse. His approach seeks to develop a framework of justice and social change and embrace emotional storytelling for the purpose of action.

In contrast to the polarising tone that is too common in political discourse, Mamdani's strategy seeks to narrow the gap by focusing on what people value and the challenges they face together. With her use of inclusive language as well as her focus on emphasising the overlooked, Mamdani's grassroots media activities help foster a sense of community and shared purpose among her constituency. By moving beyond partisan discourse, Mamdani promotes discussions that are more complex than the "either-or" divide, thus creating a culture of problem-solving and respect for each other that makes collaboration easier.

Mamdani's emphasis on grassroots organising and using common stories illustrates the value of trust and authenticity in media engagements. Instead of a top-down approach to communications, Mamdani works to invite and obtain the participation of the people he works for, acknowledging their role and the knowledge they possess in the discourse. This approach not only adds to the tapestry of voices but also fosters a spirit of buy-in and participation in the collective act of telling the stories.

Through the pooled stories from multiple voices, Mamdani seeks to construct a vision of media as a tool for social unification, a shared sense of action, and narrative democracy. His media vision goes beyond the confines of electoral campaigning by integrating the principles of social justice in media work, advocating for the decentralisation of power among the people, the inclusion of silenced narratives, the cultivation of understanding, and active, deliberative discourse.

Media Framing and Public Perception: Challenges and Opportunities

The way in which the media frames and presents stories has serious implications regarding public understanding and perception. Framing in the media refers to the construction of news stories and the highlighting and suppression of certain details, which guide an audience to a particular conclusion. This is particularly important in political discourse, as it impacts the formation of opinions, decisions, and the active participation of individuals in democracy. However, this relies on the existing power dynamics, challenges, and opportunities.

Among the challenges of media framing is the possibility of bias and misinformation. The unconscious bias or political orientation of a media house, and the ever-present financial interest, often give rise to stories that are framed to represent a certain slant. This bias and misinformation are particularly evident in the coverage of controversial issues. Additionally, the widespread presence of deliberate misinformation on social media undermines the information ecosystem. The erosion of trust in social media, along with that in public discourse, serves as evidence of this decline.

However, the process of framing presents an opportunity to tackle the issues that have come to light.

The media can improve understanding of social matters by offering differing viewpoints, placing simplistically stated issues into appropriate and sometimes complicated contexts, and verifying information. Furthermore, a deliberate attempt to add historically silenced groups and elevate stories of lesser-known issues can raise visibility of the issues and advance the overall sociocultural landscape toward an understanding that is more widening of social compassion. In this way, media framing can serve in highlighting the missing portions of the stories and bridge the gaps of the discourse.

Both policymakers and citizens should attempt to resolve media framing's creativity problems in order to make the most of the challenges and opportunities. They need to develop media literacy skills, and for the purposes of this essay, assume that this would involve the ability to analyse the credibility of an information source, identify bias, and determine whether a claim is substantiated or false, streamlining the respondents of the media information process. It is furthermore crucial to make the media environment more ethical, advocate for the stricken journalistic practice of reporting freedom, help decrease sensationalism in the media, and make the media more diverse. This should diminish the overshadowing influence of negative framing bias and raise the hallmark of elevation within the crowd.

In facing the modernisation of media communication, the social framing holds great prominence, the claiming of which rests on the ability to actively participate in the discourse, which becomes each tenth more critical. Framing the issue on behalf of social media is difficult and stifles the ethical side of the discourse. It stifles the need of a responsive population to vary, diminish, and control critical information control on behalf of the divided talked pentagon while in the hot seat.

The Role of Misinformation: Navigating Truth and Trust

Misinformation impacts democracy by changing the methodologies by which people seek and process the truth, as the intricate, paradoxical nature of truth, trust, and misinformation thickens in the age of information abundance. It is abundant and ever-present, like social media sites, a plurality of JSON feeds, hard news, news magazines, funnel reporting, and slanted kaleidoscopes of news. It lowers the public threshold of trust and the base level of discernment in the information ecosystem, deregulating the equilibria people rely upon to make contoured and coherent judgements. In the ecology of democratic information, misinformation skilfully draws attention and quickly proliferates in newsrooms and soft news pipelines, leaving the critical information to wither. A plethora of information and lack of control over its volume make retrievability almost impossible. Matcher arguments and information bearers, when uncontextualised, dynamically confusing, and available with minimal friction, actively decimate reasoning ability in their fracture zone, obliterating steps of scepticism, inquiry, and civility. They decouple people from the practised setting of objective and disciplined discourse. They dissolve the practised profession of information of truth, reason, and rigorous judgements. Addressing misinformation is a microcosm of the suburbs of the multiverse, which need the fostering of evidence-informed and critical thinking applied to every information ecosystem over facts, creative inroads to trustworthy reporting and publishers, skilful synthesis of critical trust, incisive deconstruction of silos of uncontextualised speakers and readers, and reconstruction of mutual reasoned information flows. Information untrained in the muscular discipline of scepticism becomes unmoored, pieces of reasoning, deciphering, climbing abstraction levels, and exercising intent tangled in sycophantic arms of the reattributing and diffusing masters, matchmaking reason and truth, reattributing misinformation to silos, and diffusing sense to a world thick with senseless. Active systems of boundary spanning embrace those mythical silos. Society inhales those shoulder-high democracy-ecosystem fragments, and in exchange, people exhale soft-functioning silos of uncritical thinking. Erosion sets in; truth was, and is, elastic, buoyant, and unmapped. It is asked to speak into alcohol, a bottle with sails for soft, braking instabilities of virtue, then crumbled.

With the ability to manipulate public perception and sway decisions, disorder fundamentally contradicts the structures of democracy, which media institutions must acknowledge and defend. This part attempts to unpack the fog of disorder and disinformation, presenting the case for the strengthening of the ability of the public to manage information and disinformation.

Mainstream Media's Coverage, Analysis, and Control

The influence of mainstream media on politics is very strong. As traditional news outlets continue their expansion and deepen their penetration into the audience, they fully tend to dominate in the construction of basic outlines and shaping the contexts concerning the persons and policies in politics. However, such influence does have controversy. Most commonly, the coverage, critique, and control considerations of an editorial structure's stance concerning biases an outlet possesses usually accompany more mainstream media scrutiny. Coverage: Mediacentric issues do structure the politics of an issue. Seemingly, some policies should be constructed just like tailored suits. It is an almost bound insistence for editors to modify postal to cover specific narratives, construct elites, change shares, vary dials to ascribe to, and so forth from political-correctness nonsense. These drastic headcase zeros serve to embolden editorial outcomes and indeed boost the self-consumption rate of nonsense like bored paradigm ripples. Critique: Analysis of given issues rises with equal arguments as those for cover. Each political actor is virtuously deemed as being overstepped by powerful and dominating media outlets aimed to construct a humble eagle for the entire common populace. The critique of the media itself can be determined by the public's wolfshead zeal and the corporate monopoly of the media system, together with advertising income. The perceived objectivity of such critique underscores the necessity of clarifying the matters of control. Concentration of ownership and control of the media indexically regulates the range and heterogeneity of views and voices available in the so-called mass media. The crowded marketplace of corporate and media ownership in pursuit of profit focuses the available media content and the range of viewpoints excluded, within a 'bought' context, to a barely sufficient and welcoming portrayal of dissent, marginalised, and 'othered' views. Such control raises doubts about the authenticity of the media in serving the public interest as a barometer of the problems and concerns of society. Consequently, the media's influence can be discussed only with regard to the imbalance of power in the system and the biases in the coverage, critique, and control. It is only through consideration and the construction of a cogent argument in defending such viewpoints that the range of the unaccountable and the inclusivity of the mainstream media's influence can be elucidated.

The Use of Social Media as a Democratic Tool

The benefits that governance has been exposed to as a result of the adoption of social media platforms, especially regarding communication, are unmatched, as the same platforms, especially the popular ones, have culminated in the rise of divisions within society. It has availed the opportunity of a wider scope of engaging in dialogues through social networking, which has enabled direct communication between the general public and policymakers. It has also enabled grassroots advocacy by democratically supporting weak movements which have challenged the existing hierarchies and struggled to win. It has radically shifted the manner in which political activists operate through the use of social networks, highlighting the power of social media as a tool of democracy. On the other hand, the rise of social media and the overall use of the internet have grown in a more drastic manner, as the challenges which come along with their use have also grown. The absence of any limitations on the use of social media has an alarming and uncontrollable increase in discord, which as a result weakens the standards of public discourse. The content that circulates the social media platforms is often biased, which reinforces, to a greater extent, the existing concepts of assonance and negatively affects the processes of reconciliation. Thus, the use of social media increases the possibility of a democratised society, which in return increases the possibility of social discord. Further to that, social media's ability to shape public opinions has raised questions about the credibility and nature of the information posted on various social networking sites.

The rate at which stories spread on social media especially impacts policy and public opinion. Political players and social interests use social media to shape stories and perceptions and to garner support for a cause. Users interact on these platforms in a way that enables them to react to events as they happen in a bid to shape the conversation, which may alter policy. Understanding social media as a tool for democracy requires an analysis of social media, participatory democracy and societal polarisation. The refined understanding of the use of social media stems from amalgamating its impact on public engagement and the absence of control of the information, which may cause harm. As public policy begins to accept social media's role in the broader framework of democracy, clearer issues of the balance of democracy, media control, and media policy ethics emerge. Ensuring participants and non-participants in social media democracy engage as thoughtfully as possible is the most difficult aspect of public social media use.

Impact of the Media on the Formulation of Policy and the Attitude of the People

It is evident that the media does shape the opinion of the public on various issues of politics and outcomes of various public policies formulated and executed. Studying the contrast between the approaches of Donald Trump andMohammed Mamdani on the use of the media lets us appreciate the various methods of communication and the methods of understanding the formulation of policies. Trump mastered the use of social media, and particularly Twitter, to reach out and communicate with his target audience; he avoided mainstream news processes. Trump was able to communicate his ideas without the filter of the news. This is how Trump was able to 'Tame the Trump'. Supported numerous headlines characterised the public on how to think. This was proved and depicted by subtle tweets that provoked the attention of the people to focus on the ideas that Mahmoud Trump was presenting to them. As a case in point, Mohammed Mamdani has employed the grassroots model of media engagement where the emphasis is on community narrative and mobilisation. Through community media and other local platforms, Mamdani has attempted to build personal and substantive relationships with constituents, raising the everyday American narrative and stressing issues on the grassroots agenda. This focus on bottom-up participatory and community media has created a sense of community ownership and empowerment on the issues he champions, which are very often the silenced voices of the communities he represents.

Assessing the impact of the two media strategies on policy and public opinion paints a different picture. At times, Trump's divisive and dramatic policy centred on silencing and removing public discourse on policy, attempting to reframe the discourse to drag out counter-responses with which his administration's policy agenda has been responsive to. In contrast, Mamdani has been able to amplify under-represented voices of the community media, which have been previously neglected in the public domain, and has been able to spawn bottom-up movements to change the public policy process to a more participatory approach. Mamdani's more community engagement approach, devoid of the overdramatised buzz, has enabled him to build durable, personal ties with constituents to the extent that he is able to mobilise them to participate in the policy discourse, which in turn has contributed to deepening democracy.

This analysis highlights the varying effects that the engagement with media has on the policies and public opinion, and the different ways in which such effects may occur in shaping public understanding and informing policies and governance systems. Understanding the nexuses between media tactics and political strategies proves that these forms of communication are crucial in the public sphere, giving the media the ability to maintain the status quo or unleash its potential as a transformative force.

Conclusion: The Future of Media in Political Discourse

The advanced state of media in political discourse today has brought with it serious challenges as well as available opportunities. Technology has the potential to revolutionise the spread and consumption of information in a society where political communication knows no bounds. It is no doubt now that the state of media is a determining factor of what is to come in the health and vigour of people's democracy. Media in sociopolitical life is a powerful conveyor of public opinion as well as a constructor and changer of policies. It is of enormous significance to study the way media changes have and will change in the sphere of political discourse.

One factor that needs further investigation is how misinformation and disinformation have become widespread in our digital environment. The ability of fake news and other distorted and tampered narratives to simultaneously make us lose trust in the media and disrupt public conversations is alarming. Therefore, the increasing focus on the need to counter misinformation and media disinformation and actively engage citizens in the digital space is undoubtedly of great importance.

Moreover, the contrasting tactics of politicians, for example, the ex-president's unfiltered use of social media and Mamdani's grassroots focus on bottom-up storytelling, shed light on the complex relationship of the media used in our politics today. These differing approaches highlight the relationship between old and new media, raising new questions about how each is used to encourage active and broad-based participation.

Proactively controlling the growing polarisation and echo chambers on the internet is vital for the future use of media in political discourse. These goals will also help educate the electorate. Civil discourse paired with factually accurate reporting and varied opinion will help ease the societal divides. And the ethics of availability data and privacy, the proprietary control of web-based media, and the media ownership concentration in the hands of a few companies require even greater ethical control about transparency and accountability.

The fundamental objectives of democracy include ensuring freedom of speech and silence. The media used to promote the active and responsible participation of citizens in the political processes, which would then aim – would the media, used in a transformative manner, bring to all partisans greater democracy unifying the interests of diversity? For democracy to be richer and the cross, for all, with the use of a great global attitude will promote the discipline of all media focused on moral usage toward inclusion, which will serve the public interest. It will enrich the fabric of media discourse and the focus of democracy.

9
Winning and Governing
Their Electoral Strategies and Governing Philosophies

Prelude to Power: Assessing Campaign Structures and Tactics

Studying each person's campaign structures and tactics reveals the myriad circumstances that brought each to their own version of power. In the case of Donald Trump, that mastery had to be accompanied by a command of the art of attention grabbing coupled with modern mastery of media. His unfiltered and overblown self-advertising helped him to receive and retain the attention of many who had not been recognised in the political and business environment. The strategic deployment of social media, almost entirely Twitter, helped him disintermediate the traditional media of information. He went straight to the voter. His approach made him the darling of the disaffected voters, who believed that mainstream politics had become exhausted.

In contrast, the campaign approach of someone like Mamdani was predicated on community organising and mobilising from the grassroots. His campaign was underpinned by a strategy of coalition building and engagement with the local power structure to amplify the voices of the oppressed. Rather than relying on the traditional top-down, mass media-driven approach, this strategy was designed to build support from the grassroots, with a stronger emphasis on interaction and interaction structures.

Each campaign is framed within the context of financial resources. Trump's independence and flexibility were unencumbered because he was able to self-fund a large portion of his campaign. Few other candidates had the same advantage.

Mamdani's campaign was financed through a web of small donations and volunteers who understood and practised grassroots empowerment and community-based transformative action.

Equally important is the way each candidate's rhetoric framed his campaign. Trump's brash and often reckless remarks had the effect of wildly energising his supporters while inviting withering fire from his detractors. This created a love-it-or-hate-it spectacle which was deeply polarising. Mamdani took a different approach by maintaining a carefully crafted unifying narrative that sought to bring many fractured and diverse societies together toward a common purpose of advancement and equity.

This examination of campaign frameworks and strategies is telling of how proactively and strategically each candidate sought to influence his path to power. The duel between populist exhibitionism and community-centric activism was a lesson in the plurality of options to achieve political prominence. This contributed to a richer understanding of the many intricacies involved in winning a political office.

Fireside Chats vs Viral Tweets: A Study of Communication Strategies

Every leader today is expected to engage with the public, and effective communication is crucial in accomplishing that. Populist rhetoric and democratic socialism communicate differently, and their use of the same media shows how each approach customises discourse, mobilisation, and governance. Fireside chats and viral tweets are two examples in the same domain and illustrate the differences in styles of leaders with opposing ideologies.

President Franklin D. Roosevelt branded the era of fireside chats with his radio speeches. This form of communication was used to unite the nation through a feeling of togetherness and was supposed to brace the nation in times of turmoil. The same sense of unity is supposed to be invoked through empathy. In contrast, his successors in the age of viral tweets, on the other hand, have a very different purpose: their messaging is supposed to be impactful, and that is the only bragging right that is needed from the 'traditional media' that they leap over. While tweets and radio speeches communicate the same message, the difference is that the radio speeches are supposed to build a sense of security, and the tweets have the objective of being a stream of consciousness that the audience can engage in.

The entirety of both communication techniques does not just venture into stylistic elements but leads to a more systematic approach to leadership.

Fireside chats have a more personal and thoughtful manner with which decisions and policies are formed and reasons why. On the other hand, the essence of a viral tweet captures a rush to judgement and the unrestrained ability to inform and express critical views, and a rush to action with no courtesy given to the audience. Each leader structures the tools and mediums of communication that are available to them to highlight and strengthen his or her public image, which extends to the underlying narrative of their style and effectiveness of governance.

The importance of strategies of this nature requires a more subtle analysis of their effects on and evaluations by distinct groups of people. Fireside chats, for instance, often tried to address the "big tent" by fostering empathy and social bonding across social and class divides, while viral tweets function in echo chambers and algorithmic bubbles where they sometimes deepen polarisation and tribalism but also offer a direct line to the most enthusiastic supporters. Thus, the continual advancement of the use of communication affords the digital age in particular new sets of opportunities for engagement, but also for the spread of digital falsehoods and divisiveness; the role of communication in politics becomes more complicated.

The people in charge have the difficult task of figuring out the balance and tension between the two opposing sets of processes of engagement and misunderstanding. The balance shifts for a very different reason. The very competition for the two opposed processes becomes a different opportunity for politics to work toward common outcomes as represented in the very constrained model described earlier. Picking between the two words, 'fireside chats' and 'tweets', captures the essence of a very different civilisation in the world and the polarised ideology coming out of the echoing democracies of the world. It also illustrates that in politics, as in the current age, the means becomes the very message itself.

Practising Populism: The Use of Narratives

Practising populism goes beyond just speaking. It is about making people buy into a story. Politicians like Trump and Mamdani are masters at doing this. It is important to note that there are deep grievances within these communities that are shrinking. The issue of populism has always been about tactics—how to be woven in and spark action within such disparate groups of people. To promote the entrepreneurship, political, and social energising of the "been left behind" population, Trump's supporters positioned him as a political "outsider" who fundamentally opposes elites. This "rally the base" strategy proudly gains followers and strokes political violence framed in terms of feeling empowered. It is "us" versus "them". In the same vein, Mamdani has sought to organise at the bottom and teach people to speak for themselves in the context of systemic violence and injustice. His advocacy wakes up those who are silent about injustice and domination as a payment to an ungrateful social order. Trump and Mamdani are the same in that they all use the same political, social, and economic injustice. They vigorously organise followers through media and social events, showing how important passions and hopes are in growing the movement. However, these movements are worrying about the impact they have. The populist movements have a tendency to deepen the existing social division in a society.

By using tactics aimed at inducing anger and fear, populist leaders employ nativism, irrational hostility, and anti-intellectualism to frame discussions in such a way as to make rational discussions and reasoned cooperation difficult to achieve. Furthermore, the very survival of populist movements depends on the ability to maintain a constant state of dissatisfaction—the dissatisfaction of the masses directed at the elites and others—as a means of avoiding the complex problems in a sustainable manner. As we consider the political landscapes these competing visions will produce, the complexities of the art of mobilising the populace will be crucial in the democracy and governance of the new order.

Democratic Socialism Defined: Ideals into Policy Proposals

As embraced by Mamdani, democratic socialism involves a complex vision of society in which the economy is distributed and organised by collective action and democratic control of the commanding heights. The government is charged with the responsibility of ensuring that every person, irrespective of social class, enjoys access to basic fundamental rights and freedoms such as healthcare, education, and adequate housing. It seeks to eradicate the systemic barriers that promote and sustain inequities and aims to empower and uplift the marginalised and disadvantaged through equity and justice.

Proposed policies that cultivate Medicare for All, tuition-free public college, social rights for workers, and subsidised social programmes funded through a progressively structured tax system, along with the policies that democratic socialists advocate for, seem to lean towards the imposition of a democratic social order. Providing equitable access to social resources, protecting social rights, and increasing citizen participation in governance through democratic rights is paramount.

The promotion of democratic socialism is the focus of this model, along with the emphasis on local and community-driven initiatives. Individual and collective social responsibilities through democratic progressive policies that uphold the values of human rights are the fundamental social pillars within which democratic socialism seeks to cultivate.

Strengthened bonds of social cooperation, recognition of diversity, and progressive social growth within the community are the values that democratic socialism seeks to promote through society.

Most critics of this model of governance express concerns about the financial burden associated with the effective implementation of the policies. Others argue that social investment in social and human development will likely improve social and economic productivity. This model will also assist in alleviating social injustices and structural disparities that have existed in society for centuries.

Mamdani's advocacy for democratic socialism examines its practicality, probing how such principles can become policy to rectify justice gaps and foster empathy in society. Ideals and implementable principles are not typically studied together, and this is where Mamdani sheds light on the reconfiguration of governance for the transformative potential that change can offer to all citizens.

The Ground Game: Grassroots Movements and Field Operations

Like other elements of a campaign, grassroots movements and field operations are fundamental to its success. These features highlight the level of dedication a candidate has relative to the electorate. This section addresses an important dimension of campaign strategies, particularly the nuanced activities integral to the campaign's grassroots engine.

Part of a campaign's success hinges on the relentless dedication of volunteers and organisers to canvassing, phone banking, and holding other community engagement events and activities designed to build personal relationships with the target electorate. These relationships are important in candidate-voter issue identification and validation dynamics. This understanding captures the feeling of 'real democracy', where the citizen's needs are not just glossed over but actually engaged with in the most humane way possible.

Furthermore, field operations are not just limited to conventional outreach, as there are new ways to mobilise supporters and expand campaign horizons. With the help of digital and social media, activists are able to reach and mobilise wider audiences for online advocacy and to amplify the campaign's message on an unprecedented scale. Campaigns that integrate face-to-face outreach and online organising are able to reach and engage a broad cross-section of the population while increasing their campaign's visibility in the noise of contemporary communication.

Another important feature of the ground game is the planned allocation of resources and personnel. Campaigns meticulously strategise the mapping of precincts, the allocation of volunteers, and the placing of sponsored advertisements in order to enhance engagement and impact. Using advanced analytics and predictive modelling, campaign managers pinpoint strategic opportunities and allocate resources for increased support and turnout to maximise engagement in targeted communities. This ensures an optimal approach to community engagement and shows the level of efficiency in resource allocation.

Moreover, authentic engagement with local leaders and grassroots organisations cultivates synergistic relationships that strengthen the campaign's visibility and reputation in the target community. Campaigns that collaborate with prominent spearheads strategically target grassroots organisations to access a wider community, gain sponsorships, and enhance their collective impact in message dissemination and ground mobilisation.

The ground game eloquently describes the life of democracy as consisting of human relationships and technology and purposeful arrangements designed to mobilise and effect change at the community level. It is a complete participatory democracy of the people, giving voice to the common citizen and emphasising the importance of civic engagement. In any campaign, the key lies in the cultivation of this movement and the direction of its momentum to design a future resonant with the will of the people.

Strategic Management: Building the 'Public Image'

Strategic management involves creating a 'public image' which is tremendously different from simply putting on a cheerful or sympathetic 'mask'. Rather, it involves a meticulously crafted blend of personal traits, values, policies, and communication methods that resonate with the audience. In pursuing their goals, each of the 'subjects' of our case, Trump and Mamdani, has pursued a different strategy in trying to propagate their 'brands'.

In the case of Trump, the focus of the brand is on the public image, which is centred around an almost mythical depiction of success and total mastery over everything. Be it the trademark phrase 'You are fired' or the ostentatious display of wealth symbolised by his numerous skyscrapers and golf courses, the Trump brand is in the business of winning, and Trump himself is the ultimate trophy. He is aware of the business and, more importantly, confident enough to sponsor the image of an unyielding, blunt leader capable of solving the most intricate dimensions of big puzzles and doing so at the highest level. This, in turn, is what is appealing to his voters: the fact that he is a bold and confident leader that never backs down.

Rather, it is based on authenticity, empathy, and grassroots connection on which Mamdani builds his public image. He has managed to sustain the image of an accessible and empathetic leader who understands and promotes the issues of the people because of his community organising and advocacy. He is a transparent, accountable, and inclusive person, which sets him apart because he is willing to help the marginalised and empowers individuals to feel powerful.

These media engagements are important when it comes to the construction of these public images. For example, Trump has used mainstream and social media to send his messages directly to the audience. His aggressive and open approach positions him as the centre of attention and allows him to control the news, ensuring his constant relevance. In the case of Mamdani, he used grassroots advocacy, community action and the internet to promote himself as a leader of democracy who favours egalitarianism and participatory governance.

In addition, the appearance branding of a leader requires both the careful tailoring of speeches that capture its essence and the creation and repurposing of meaning in signage and brand visuals of the leader. While in Trump's case he has catchy phrases and chain-like 'slogans' like 'Make America Great Again' and supporting imagery like red baseball caps, for Mamdani the campaign's triadic themes of justice, equity, and solidarity provide the framework. The imagery that each leader evokes—Trump's well-known Trump 'gold' motif and gold-plated everything in the White House, along with the Trump ether and shimmer—and Mamdani's cosmopolitan, thoughtfully planned town hall meetings demonstrate the disparity in their styles of engagement.

In the last paragraph, a particular character is likely to take the place of the leaders, which, to my mind, is conservative in the sense that he draws the red line of the public to the way of fabricating and endlessly artistically rewriting the storyline of himself, which is an immortal virtue of the leaders, as it has ever been. The leader does not observe the edges of the public's emotional fabric, the lines that triangulate movement, or the artwork of phantom clouds which his or her public stitch to the back to follow. The edges of fabric can reveal the intricacies of the public, which take the shapes and hues of the absent, and which, with the extreme surge of political artifice, lead a trail of them to the ladders to the brand of political art. The notion is to provide them with a sense of prim and proper virtue, which is why it is likely political art can flourish in the empty vacuum he or she outputs in public.

Let's gain an understanding of the phantoms we observe. The supporters of these leaders, who gaze blankly at the phosphorus clouds, also represent currents in society. These leaders include Mamdani, who is accompanied by a dynamic group that shapes the empty air around them, while Trump stands with clouds behind his hand, resembling polished stares similar to those that framed the television screen at Mamdani's town halls. Ward off clouds to bind barefoot to the invisible crest of a bright splash of story fabric, her fellow from his gilded enclave. Who capture the light to throw shards around a new bond, brilliant haloes. These partisan beacons, along with the one bin of creation, spill something more than the road of broken lines from the seamstresses, and fragmentation billows clutch to. These are elections; the purpose is not to gain more brightness with each flash.

The argument is about text. Words form a network that combines sense and ethos with physical strength. Their derivatives, while crosshatched, need no claim. From strands always I will share polyphonic shadows, losing matter shining not from a void but from the too close-knit fog of the dozen calls reasserting reverently the former, that each ground stirs in. He remembered the fabric in the approach. This is the soft knot; initially, it has a cool shine and emits smoke. The fabric is cast with the frames, not the backs, resembling the wrap of ancient makers as it slips along the beams. Out of every splash shining bald, a burst to coax and lamp through. The semi-permeable sonic strainer, adorned with prism edges, serves as the political watermark of the hovering multitude. The lace on my eggs and the cleavage of your shattered star line are still connected, allowing a wild, errant curve to trace back the figures and extend beyond its shimmer. Now bloom bright to resist her inside. These, my pages, are for her future. The republished content comes from the hidden thumb, featuring a red blur against a blue background. The question lurks behind her legs. Behind her legs' question, which holds.

Let me swoop from the meteors beyond. Order is what shines the brightest. Each clan in the Thumb novel uses these shapes with core light to speak and arrange wellbeing. The girls, with ink-bonder edges appearing, sang the tighter of my halos. The blue, which was too hot to handle, was wrapped in an open embrace. The replication of their mural to tell takes place frame first; each point softens, a pebble near rough, which the flash widens, the way of reflected voices and shouts.

Pull their seeds to land, and the ladle stretches to hidden seams, shining as a bright dusted border. This is a constantly evolving roughness that I experience. Like gilded spit from aeons past, light gathers and dares to stretch from one star to another. Each perfume is really the same; each is as current.

The argument is about phenomena. The quiet ways in which the rhythms of everything play are truly remarkable. The flowing fingers that cross inside each wedded shadow and the gentle dip to the soft seams in the gathered edges are both gracious, as is the zephyr-swift coil that moves through the frame to touch the artery.

Governing amid Division: Navigating Bipartisan Landscapes

In complex governing within a divided polity, understanding bipartisanship, coalition building, and the art of compromise is crucial, requiring a profound and thoughtful understanding. It is common to see how leaders in charge are met with the full formal and public opposition of the opposing side, the result of which is the unmaking of substantive elements of any given policy. This is why governing in a state of deep division requires a contextually pluralistic approach. It requires a careful understanding of the ideal approach to dividing policy options, which are fundamentally variations in structure and order.

As polarised politics advance, a comprehensive philosophy emerges that maps the underlying issues governing the policy scope of any given alignment. It examines the core elements, and for productive hands that cross the barriers of the respective parties, changes in attitude and behaviour are required.

Equally, the politics of divisions are the recognition of the fundamentally different constituents that the state holds and the different aspects of its population. It involves treating everyone with civility, ensuring that the inclusion of any group is constructive and considers all segments of the population, including partisans and others. This approach recognises that the existing pluralistic democracy aims to unite, but achieving unity through civility, respect, justice, and equality presents a separate challenge.

Effective governance is determined by the ability to devise strategies that foster cooperation across the varied ideological divides brought on by partisanship, even when obstacles arise. Diplomacy, defined by the profound understanding of the issues at hand, the willingness to empathically resolve the tension, and the skilful ability to devise the strategy needed to manoeuvre the divide, is what is needed. Realising that success can involve reaching out to the other side and listening to their grievances is crucial.

In addition, the ethical approach needed to govern amidst conflict destroys the perception of the fading importance of the divisions within society. Ethical governance continues to be the standard, with the expectation being a willingness to act based on the ethical belief that the truth must be communicated, even during the most intense conflict between opposing sides. The principle of governance involves communicating leadership expectations, which in turn fosters confidence, trust, civic engagement, and unity.

Another important aspect is appreciating the connections and interdependent parts that contribute to democracy. Empathy and the willingness to transcend the ideological divides are essential; unity of effort, harmony among the people, and practical applications of democracy can be achieved through thoughtful, desired, sustainable, and inclusive outcomes. Achieving these outcomes reflects the ability to govern, while unity depends on the capacity to effectively navigate the complex dynamics of democracy, bipartisanship, and cooperation.

Promises vs. Policies: Fulfilling Policies and Enactments

At this point, we examine the political promises and actions of both subjects and the political aspects they influenced. By examining the subjects, we analyse how difficult it is to translate political promises into practical realities within the state's decision-making echelons.

In the case of Donald Trump, he is arguably and undeniably the first American president in history who has both tried and managed to perform a tendentious set of policies in a single term, some of which are reminiscent of his pre-candidacy positions. For instance, in relation to his administration's policies of taxation and spending, there was a strong prediction that the tax reform bill would do something to alleviate the tax burden, particularly on the middle class, which in effect is an electoral promise. Nonetheless, there was strong opposition to the claim that this legislation was fiscally regressive. In another instance, his attempts to repeal and replace Obamacare were in fact more flashy, and he lost track of the most important legislation to the point where the entire four years of the Trump administration were a failure.

The completed definition of the term is as follows. In contrast, the shift to elected office has brought with it a zealous support of policies characteristic of democratic socialism. From the point of view of execution, his attempts to shift the focus on reforming healthcare, such as his advocacy of Medicare for All, and the focus on equity in housing have still been motivated by an attitude geared towards thoroughgoing change. Legislative attempts to control rent and protect tenants illustrate both the rhetoric of community empowerment and the actual enforcement of laws, clearly aligning what is hoped for with what is achieved. The attempts in this case to regulate the order of things are a testament to the challenges and complexities involved in trying to change the order in which things are governed.

Evaluating the reality of promises set against the reality of policies established is where the critical examination of power relations begins. This examines the complexities of political will, institutional limits, and the public. This dichotomy is vital for judging leaders' effectiveness and legitimacy, building their legacies, and helping voters discern fact from fiction. In the next chapters, we will investigate the socioeconomic and political impacts of the policies in question and trace the consequences of governance choice and action, especially the choice to evoke control when conflict mends the rift and opposition meets collaboration.

Assessing Impact: Political and Socio-Economic

The tension between the monopolist and the social democrat is continuously increasing. Consequently, these phenomena are accompanied by shifts in social and political dynamics. Assessing governance philosophies, including policy usage and changes in the populace's mentality, is a profound task. The social and political shifts are considerable. The complexity of governance policies extends beyond individual cases.

It is evident that the social governance influenced by populist rhetoric is customised. The basic measures, when combined with others, dictate the provision of services and the distribution of social and essential income. It primarily fortifies the intended populist and social democrat governance strategies, which comprise a disparate set of investment-focused social politics. However, the intended populist and social democrat governance strategies feature a disparate set of rational policies.

Simultaneously, assessing the ideologies' political effects is vital. It requires the study of changes in the structure of political power, the level of polarisation, political activity, the degree of openness in the political system, and the extent of pluralism. It is important to assess how each of these approaches affects democratic institutions, representation, and the public's confidence in the government. The evolution of policies, the measures of accountability, and the functions of the population's governing interests also aid in determining the more general political implications of different styles of governance.

Similarly important is the study of the interaction between socio-economic and political aspects. The interaction is between policy choices, social stratification, and the level of active participation in the democratic process. It is an analysis of the positive corollary of public policies on the economy and politics. Synthesising the socio-economic and political outcomes delineates the implications of governance that follows populist slogans and professed democratic socialism in an obvious and comprehensive manner, providing the readers a well-defined basis for comparison and an analytical framework.

A comprehensive evaluation of the socio-economic and political effects of different governing philosophies allows one to assess the legacies of leadership in a more holistic way. With this understanding, they appreciate the implications of the decision to adopt alternative means of governance, which enriches their contextual knowledge and understanding of the relationship between ideas, policies, and their implementations.

Legacy and Lessons: What Their Journeys Reveal About Power

Examining affiliated leaders with contrasting ideologies sheds light on fundamental lessons derived from power and its use in democracies. Looking at the leaders in question, it becomes clear that the application of power involves different dimensions within the parameters of leadership, reach, and the consonance of decisions as the theme becomes more complex. Donald Trump's legacy provides evidence of the advantage of leadership precision and the ability to "sell" stories to the less privileged people of the country. His term in office illustrates the extent to which political stories flourish and the omnipresence of populist discourse. On the other hand, individuals with a democratic socialist inclination inform us about the overwhelming abundance of yearning for a specific frame of reference and structural reorganisation of the social contract. Effective political discourse explains the vibrancy of movements and their instrumental roles in setting the national agenda and mobilising the populace towards a collective purpose. These divergent approaches provide important lessons on the level of interaction of an individual with society, and the lessons of an individual society on his/her use of that power tell the complete story of the change that is needed. In addition, the study of these legacies highlights the urgency and the enduring need to introduce public discourse that is more attentive to the democratic fractures and sociopolitical divisions of the world today.

Their journeys compel us to understand the unresolved tensions between wielding power and fostering equitable, sustainable progress. Therefore, the examples set by the leaders serve as a litmus test for grasping the moral and ethical factors that drive the use of influence in the modern world. They urge us to reconsider the dominant frameworks within which we consider power, responsibility, and the responsible use of public trust. Ultimately, reflecting on what their journeys teach us about power encourages us to think critically and engage in discussions on the essence and purpose of governance, permitting an enlightened and progressive approach to the exercise of power.

10
America at the Crossroads
Synthesis of Competing Visions

America's Ideological Crossroads

America is at a significant crossroads within itself, trying to deal with ideological problems that are of a particular age. The extent of ideological conflict within America has become part of the long-standing debate over the various directions this vast nation might take in the future. Issues related to governance, individual freedom, power, and politics have significantly influenced and transformed the discourse surrounding the evolution of the American way of life. Almost all of the ideological conflicts which have taken place in world history and in the arms of America have taken place in the form of the former and older political argument in the arms of America and in the world, whether Federalist and Anti-Federalist or the Civil Rights and the Question of Race in the 20th century and middle 20th century, and the world even today in terms of policies related to economy and social in all of its facets. The previous precedents have significantly influenced various aspects of how the modern American world operates. The level of American politics today tells a clear tale and is centred around major issues like America's ideological crossroads, immigration borders, defence, healthcare, global warming, wealth separation, the economy, and the increasing deficit. Over the period of time, American politics has had the capability to maintain the cross-sectional balance in the rhetoric and the policies. American politics can prevent major policies and issues that create divisions while fostering constructive dialogues for policy development.

When considering the advancement of communication technology and the introduction of social media, more intense division and reinforcing preexisting beliefs have always been accompanied by increased ideological echo chambers. With a rich history and stark contemporary divide, America, at this very moment, seems to be at an ideological crossroad, which bears far-reaching consequences for the future of the nation. This chapter seeks to explore the issues of ideological conflict in America, the roots of division and conflict, and the possible responses to such challenges.

Context: The Episodes of Ideological Conflict

The history of the United States is dotted by ideological conflicts, and the period shaped by each conflict has in turn shaped the development of the nation. The conflict and ratification of the Constitution, the Civil War that tore the Union apart, the subsequent Progressive Era reforms, and the civil rights movement of the twentieth century all constitute crucial and pivotal episodes of the American 'struggle'. 'What does America want to become?' is a question that many of these epochs wrestle with.

The philosophical clashes of the republic's founding years stemmed from the numerous attempts at delineating 'individual liberty', allocating federal power, and slavery. As for the Federalists and anti-Federalists, the clash of ideas was the midpoint of the struggle between a controlled centre and the rights of the constituent units, which was the basis for a multitude of future confrontations about governance in the United States.

A myriad of conflicting ideas were sharply illustrated in the Civil War, which took centre stage in the ideological schism, exposing the numerous divisions regarding slavery and contesting the vision for America's future. Economic interests, morals, and regional loyalty divisions sparked a profound clash with unfathomable consequences, transforming the country's social and political structure.

The Progressive Era met the social and economic challenges of hyperindustrialization head-on. Activists and reasoned thinkers challenged the capitalist notions of government non-interference, emphasising the active role democracy needed to address labour issues, impoverished communities, and capitalist monopolies. The orthodox ideas that colluded with the attempts to progress were termed 'Progressive Era', which were targeted towards every nation's right to a fairer and more equal society in legislation.

During the mid-20th century, there was ardent advocacy for civil rights and social equality for the underprivileged, including the Montgomery Boycott and the Washington March, among others. These events were significant in bringing racial injustice and a lack of equal opportunity to national attention, resonating simultaneously throughout America's power structures.

These events in our history are important, as they indicate the strong disagreements and transformations in thinking regarding the development of America, which aids in understanding the significance of conflicting thoughts in both the past and present of America.

The Trump Vision: Reimagining American Conservatism

The American political system is built on differing ideologies, primarily on the left and right. Donald Trump tends to downplay the importance of the right wing and attempts to diminish its ideologies. In Trump's view, the state's duty is to optimally embrace populist nationalism, appeasing it through assertive executive decisions, protectionism, and law and order. For Trump, and regarding his Americanization, there is nothing more paramount than the 'America First' approach to foreign relations. This conservatism is prudent without being sacrosanct. Conservative populism is exquisitely esoteric and paradoxical. In Trump's world, effective pirate capitalism exists; therefore, other left-wing figures try to justify it as they do in der Abendland. One element of Trump's vision is characterised by the use of tariffs and the transformation of the American economy as neoliberal, as well as the dismantling of the structures of American economic dominance compared to other nations. Trump is well-known for adopting the most pirate-like trade practices to support his position. His legislation on border control testifies to a belief in a propaganda state tightly controlled by Trump's left wing. It describes the practice of immigration control with severe restrictions, aimed at protecting the country behind its borders.

This continent is destined to be a boundless realm of unrestricted freedom where the caste system ladders built by other nations do not reach. It signifies a thoughtful pause in governance, allowing for the recovery and replacement of previous leaders. His positive practices reflect a belief in order and an unyielding stance against militarism. His voters and the U.S. as a whole seek to boast of restored American control in the global arena, yet they are based on soft power with self-disciplines more intricate than mere fiscal advantage policies. This reflexive, soft American dominance rests on the will to prioritise profits.

In addition to the undefined policy particulars, Trump's vision rationally targets the coveted core of nostalgic values and American industries, securing the support of working-class voters who have been disinherited and left behind by the processes of globalisation and the technological boom. This counter-narrative also possesses an anti-establishment angle, portraying Trump as an alternative to the political status quo. Trump has made efforts to reshape America through the assumption of the federal government's abdication, the implementation of conservatively orientated taxes, and the promotion of government-sponsored ethics of personal exceptionalism and an individualistic economy. The proposed 'shaping' of conservatism has, in turn, led to fierce and uncontrollable hostility in the form of criticism regarding authoritarianism and inflationary and xenophobic attitudes. It goes without saying that Trump's vision has fundamentally reshaped and restated the geography of conservatism in America. Most importantly, it has shifted and unsettled the political discourse in America, while also extending a call for the boundaries of political imagination, especially within the Republican Party and across the country.

Mamdani's Optics: Transformative Progression

Mamdani sees himself as a defender of transformative progress aligned with social justice and economic equity within the radical Trumpian vision of American conservatism. His vision for the future of America evolves by investing all energies in confronting systemic injustice and advocating for the social and economic uplift of the marginalised. Mamdani's vision is a bold explanation for the gross social injustice. He argues for transformative equity. He believes in the redistribution of wealth in addition to universally accessible education, healthcare, and affordable housing. Change, in the socio-economic order of America predominantly influenced by capitalist structures, is what is radical and transformational in Mamdani's advocacy.

Mamdani's transformative progress consists of a radical vision concerning the historical injustices with a willingness to address them through interventional policies. It is framed with an empathetic and moral consciousness, in a vision that contrasts with policies that perpetuate inequality and oppression. It is essential to understand the aims of Mamdani, who seek to change the racial, economic, and political injustices that marginalise a predominantly sunk, inner-reputable society that stretches to the centre of the perched ecosystem of democracy. It is America for them.

Mamdani goes beyond policies on the table; he advocates for a complete rethink of the values that underpin America. His imaginative advocacy for change goes against the current 'gospel' of individualism and meritocracy and draws attention to the importance of solidarity and community.

Closing the circle of success of a society to the prosperity and dignity of the society's most marginalised members, Mamdani aims to build a nation that is inclusive and caring and that recognises the interdependence of its people.

Mamdani goes on to advocate that the pursuit of social justice should, in fact, be considered a pathway for advancing the nation's interests, and not a diversion from it. By combining justice, compassion, and sound policies, he attempts to shift the frame of American politics and social life. In relation to what is currently considered mainstream conservative thought, his is a refreshing proposition that aims to provide equitable and sustainable outcomes for all people in America.

Shared Challenges: Economic Inequality and Social Justice

Mamdani's advocacy for clear policies to mitigate social injustice stems from the enduring inequities and anger that imbalances in wealth and income inequality can create. Today, inequality in wealth, income, and even the opportunities available to people sparks discontent, and in America these economic inequities serve to divide and isolate. People believe that inequality can serve as the fundamental basis for political mobilisation. Coupled with this vision rests social justice. An unequal society, after all, is a misguided democracy. Thus, what is needed are democracy and social justice policies that elevate the underprivileged, eliminate systemic marginalisation, and ensure equitable distribution of resources and opportunities. His social justice policies integrate him into the broader structural reflexive actions taken by the progressive movement for social and economic justice, which seeks to democratise and securitise the social and economic relationships of the citizens. On the contrary, Trump was the first political leader to advocate the application of market-orientated, deregulatory policies that assert the economy grows strong and robust for the society's hidden benefits. Detractors of this vision have vigorously argued that his policies have only sharpened the existing inequality and have failed to uplift the poor. In this case, competing visions of wellbeing and justice for marginalised people and the rest of society are mostly shaped by the answers they give to economic inequality.

Social justice encompasses not only addressing economic inequalities but also filling the gaps in the American discrimination and bigotry landscape. The types of discrimination that are crucial to address in discussions about bigotry include racism, sexism, and homophobia, which undermine justice and equality. People like Mamdani focus on eradicating bigotry through civil policies, increasing civil rights defenders, and advancing inclusion structures. All these together help shift the power balance in historically neglected communities. On the other hand, the social justice implications of Trump's rhetoric and policy actions have incurred many controversies, which leads to the question of whether his presidency supports or further strains social justice policies. The divide on economic and social justice issues is seamless and is central to America, whether in the office or in his prison stripes. It reveals the struggle that America faces in wanting to overcome its backwardness and move forward while reconciling its social justice issues with its founding principles. These principles form the foundation of a vision for America, created by those who are competing and including themselves in shaping its future.

Crossing Cultural Borders: Identity and Inclusion

America is currently grappling with a deeply divided cultural landscape that centres on issues of identity and inclusion. The intersection of multiple races, religions, and economic demographics has created significant diversity; however, it has also led to troubling divisions and societal friction, which Donald Trump and Mamdani address in their works. His unique background and future aspirations lend weight to both ends of the spectrum. Part of Trump's strategy has unfortunately worked against the goal of American integration, serving to exalt certain identities while placing others in a state of 'otherness'. Mamdani's work, in contrast, is based on the principles of inclusivity and acknowledgement of the diverse identities that make up America. Mamdani's community organising work showcases his commitment to empowering marginalised individuals, thereby transforming the narrative of who matters and who belongs. This chapter examines how these strategies and their consequences impact the lives of people and communities in the country as a whole. The chapter focuses on how cultural frameworks impact identity and inclusivity and the resulting impact on social affinity and community welfare.

The chapter discusses the impact of cultural disparities on state cohesion and the potential for bridging these divides amid increasing polarisation. Through the disparate perspectives of Trump and Mamdani, this section attempts to shed light on the intricate issues of the conflicts of identity and affiliation in the current American society, attempting to address the depth of the social division and the unity needed and the means to achieve it. The readers are left to contemplate the personal disposition towards these cultural gaps and the manner in which they can contribute towards building a more understanding and compassionate society.

Institutional Responses: The Resilience of Democracy

The resilience of democracy is tested by the strength of its institutions during ideological battles and conflicts within society. The United States' system of government is based on the separation of democratic norms and principles at both the federal and state levels. There is an executive, legislative, and judicial branch on both the state and local levels. Each of these institutions has undergone significant stress testing in the past years, but their durability and ability to adapt speak to the strength of democracy in America.

One of the aspects of the resiliency of democracy is the existence of the absence of war. The absence of war is the consequence and condition of the system of 'positive peace' developed to prevent the erosion of authoritarian rule. The system of 'positive peace' focuses on nurturing friendly, reciprocal, and supportive ties among civic groups. The building of such ties is to make democracy decision-making easier because the system tries to prevent any one individual, or group, from dominating the entire process.

In addition, the value of an independent judiciary in

democracy's construction, and even its defence, cannot be exaggerated. The courts, as constitutionally mandated and unencumbered by political interferences, and as guardians of the constitution, serve as an important bulwark against the possible excesses of the other arms of government. The demonstration of adherence to the rule of law in these cases through decisions that sustain and protect the essence of democracy even in politically heated cases strengthens the durability of democracy.

At the same time, civil society, which comprises advocacy networks, charitable organisations, and other grassroots movements, serves as an important point of contact for citizens and the polity. By articulating and facilitating the active participation of citizens, as well as in the processes of demand and supply of accountability to government representatives, these structures enhance the independent working of democracy. Their capacity to mobilise public opinion, heal the fractures in society, and construct public policies that are responsive to democracy augment the claim and the working of democratic institutions.

Nevertheless, while solid institutions provide the foundation upon which the resilience of a democracy rests, they are still not exempt from attempts at systemic challenges or subversion. Factors such as the politics of polarisation, the monetisation of politics, and targeted disinformation campaigns are significant threats to the workings of democracy within any society. Confronting such threats requires vigilance, reform aimed at increasing accountability and transparency, and a re-dedication to the principles at the heart of the democratic cause.

At the same time that the country is grappling with its own ideological crossroads, it is critical to understand

and strengthen the institutional responses to underpin resilience that approaches democracy as a system of governance. America will be able to steer through its politically turbulent waters and work towards greater unity and inclusion if it defends and strengthens the spine of its democratic system.

Public Euphoric Opinions: Bipolarisation and Unifying Values

Public sentiment in America has reached a stage of deep division that reflects a troubling set of bipolar attitudes characteristic of the nation's citizenry. Indeed, the public's opinion on healthcare, immigration, and the social and economic inequalities of government action has shifted. And though ease of discussion and the accepted norm of straightforwardness lead some to frame this as a simple difference of opinion, it is much more profound in nature. There is discord, anger, and touchiness on the questions and assertions that relate to the subject. The outcome is a sort of gross domestic conflict and societal discord.

Amid the apparent flaws in reason and logic in this conflict, and perhaps in the stark absence of touchstones, the discord did give way to unison and a common set of values. Indeed, people in the country, despite the forks of division that the media has largely dominated, do sincerely wish to join in unison, collaborate, and progress. It is paramount that the discourse emanating from such values is put on a much wider platform, replaced with reason.

Moreover, one is compelled to learn the root causes of

societal division. These are the discords arising from economic disparity, a greater cultural rift, and lack of access to important historical information. The touchstone of this division can, if understood deeply, be the absence of frame and structure to the discourse passer and its intended points in it.

Fostering common ground is not about the imposition of unanimity, nor the surrender of the pillars of one's principles. It rather means the creation of environments that allow for discourse that is constructive and civil. Discourse of this kind is characterised as inquiry on the part of participants from divergent backgrounds about points of common interest that might be shared. Interaction of this sort has the capabilities, whether within community assemblies, on social networks, or within the political arena, to close wide gulfs of differences and foster solidarity.

Providing amphitheatre discourse that is constructive and seamless discussion for the purpose of hospitality, which is a decisive concern of the congregational assembly, brings out the common ground that intersects at the junction of hospitality and common ground. The participants, for the purpose of reconciliation, whose polarised structures of society are envisaged to be enfolded within the positive embrace of.

Explaining Reciprocal analysis of the sequence of feelings, the complexity of emotions, and the layer of the public is able to internalise the essence which lies within the atmosphere that is evocative, formative, and nurturing. Embracing and caring within the arena of discourse on civic corresponding rubrics, touching the desire and wish to respect differences, most rounded in steps which disassemble partisans would like to see distant from.

Potential Outcomes: Scenarios for the Future

When analysing the possible outcomes of the ideological conflict at the heart of American politics, it is necessary to consider multiple potential outcomes for both the near and distant future. One outcome, for instance, would be ongoing polarisation. Polarisation, which is the social and political division between differing visions, would increase tension regarding competing notions. This would most certainly strengthen the concept of echo chambers, tribalism, and, of course, the search for mutual interests or understanding. It would further lead to stagnated policies that would hinder the nation from succeeding in resolving important issues. Another possible outcome is a form of polarisation that leans more towards moderation, thus both sides having to accept that they need to begin to search for mutual resolutions. This would hopefully renew the spirit of 'what is best for the country' and bipartisanship, leading to constructive communication to create the much-needed and desired landmark legislation for America. It's that or some type of reframing ideological disruptor or transformative leader. Something that may be a wonder of the world, like technology, or a shift in geopolitics.

Such an event would indeed strip away some of the fundamental ideological layers of the debate, encouraging new forms of political partnerships while dismantling the political structures that currently exist. Still, the development of this kind of transformative outlier is entirely uncertain and unpredictable. Moreover, the grimmer scenario concerns the proliferation of conflict and violence in society. The crossfire of ideas, which is poorly managed, generates tornadic civil unrest and aids the disintegration of all the values upon which democracy rests. In this disorientated social architecture, the hope for rational discussion and compromise becomes increasingly unlikely, which terribly undermines the fabric of social integration and peace that the country needs. In the end, the ideological warfare possesses unpredictable consequences, which are of an intricate nature and require ample consideration in decision-making. Where America goes, this configuration of mappable and also unpredictable outcomes is rooted in the actions and choices and the part that citizens, together with the authority and the framework of the country, are willing to step forward towards the pragmatic issues and multifarious options lying ahead.

Conclusion: Further Steps in a Still-Polarised America

This book has shown that a stark example of the ideological divisions that exist in America can be found in the stark differences in the worldviews of Trump and Mamdani. Those differences represent wider divides in the economic, social, and cultural fabric of the nation. Yet, amid this chaos, there lies the possibility of a unifying, albeit difficult, path that strives to bring the country to a state of unity, equity, and progress. The way forward is undoubtedly anchored by pragmatism that holds tightly to the values that America stands for, while also understanding the complicated nature and intricacies of the problems at hand. It is a move away from the status quo of defending partisan loyalty to a willing advocacy for real negotiation and agreement.

A way forward is the recognition that both sides of the American progressive and conservative spectra deal with real issues, which, in their totality, need addressing. From there, the fusion of those ideologies has the potential to produce multifaceted solutions which the country desperately needs. The solutions for the new America need to emerge from some form of cooperation that transcends the dilatory thinking associated with target-centric politics. In other words, we need a new, vibrant, and active type of politics that is rooted in the principle of active civility and encourages the type of engagement that is fair-minded: where informing, supporting, and working together come to the forefront, rather than triumphing, rejoicing, and disdain.

Finally, moving forward requires a more effective approach to addressing inequalities and injustices that foster marginalisation and division that go deeper than the surface. It involves narrowing the economic, racial, and social democratic gaps through targeted and inclusive policies and programmes that support and uplift disadvantaged groups and attempt to remedy the injustice of history. It is of utmost importance in achieving social cohesion and a fairer, more inclusive, and equitable democratic society that the country recognises and embraces diversity as an important asset and a foundational element of national identity.

How pivotal leadership is to forging that path cannot be emphasised enough. All leaders, regardless of their political affiliation, must rise above polarisation and ideological blindness to put the common good over partisan interests. This requires a departure from inflammatory rhetoric to the practice of governance that is inclusive, respectful, and responsive to the needs of all the people. It requires ethical, uncompromising, and principled leadership characterised by openness and a willingness to unite the country by guiding her towards national reconciliation and common prosperity.

The course to take in this divided America depends heavily on the readiness of people, communities, and even organisations to seek out and overcome divisions, understand and defend democracy and justice, and face the challenges that lie ahead. The country's polarisation can be overcome, and the advancement of unity, justice, and shared wealth can be achieved if people work together and imagine a tomorrow that is collaborative, inclusive, and resilient.

www.ingramcontent.com/pod-product-compliance
Lightning Source LLC
Chambersburg PA
CBHW051544020426
42333CB00016B/2090